University of East Anglia

PROSE FICTION

MA Creative Writing
Anthologies 2014

UEA PROSE FICTION ANTHOLOGY 2014

First published by Egg Box Publishing 2014

International ©2014 retained by individual authors

This book is sold subject to the condition that it shall not, by way of trade or otherwise, be lent, resold, hired out, stored in a retrieval system, or otherwise circulated without the publisher's prior consent in any form of binding or cover other than that in which it is published and without a similar condition including this condition being imposed on the subsequent purchaser.

A CIP record for this book is available from the British Library.

UEA Prose Fiction Anthology 2014 is typeset in Caslon. Titles are set in Din condensed, with subtitles in Gotham.

Printed and bound in the UK by Imprint Digital.

Designed and typeset by Sean Purdy.

Proofread by Sarah Gooderson.

Distributed by Central Books.

ISBN: 9780957661158

ACKNOWLEDGEMENTS

Thanks are due to the School of Literature, Drama and Creative Writing at UEA in partnership with Egg Box Publishing for making this anthology possible.

We'd also like to thank the following people:

Trezza Azzopardi, Amit Chaudhuri, Andrew Cowan, Giles Foden, Sarah Gooderson, Lavinia Greenlaw, Rachel Hore, Kathryn Hughes, James Lasdun, Daniel Leeson, Michael Lengsfield, Frances Leviston, Jean McNeil, Natalie Mitchell, Beatrice Poubeau, Sophie Robinson, Helen Smith, Henry Sutton, Val Taylor, Steve Waters, Peter Womack and Toby Young.

Nathan Hamilton at Egg Box Publishing and Sean Purdy.

Editorial team:

Michelle Brown
Susan K Burton
Niall Cunniffe
John Dennehy
Hannah Coneys
Affly Johnson
Ella Micheler
Lauren Razavi
Anealla Safdar
Rebecca White

And with thanks to Jacqueline Landey, Lily Meyer and Sophia Veltfort.

CONTENTS

Foreword
Anjali Joseph—09

Introduction
Jean McNeil and Henry Sutton—11

Contributors
Ayobami Adebayo—13

Joe Banfield—19

Julia Breens—25

Mark Chaiken—31

Dave Chua—37

Krishan Coupland—43

Alice Falconer—47

Rory Gleeson—53

Imogen Hermes Gowar—59

Kate Gwynne—**63**

Liz Hambrick—**69**

Nick Kipley—**75**

Jacqueline Landey—**81**

Elspeth Latimer—**87**

Ferdia Lennon—**93**

Isa Lorenzo—**99**

John Patrick McHugh—**105**

Lily Meyer—**111**

Ng Yi-Sheng—**117**

Nicolas Padamsee—**123**

Dani Redd—**131**

Emma Rhind-Tutt—**137**

Jess Roussos—**143**

Anealla Safdar—**149**

Poppy Sebag-Montefiore—**155**

Nick Shadowen—**161**

Sophia Veltfort—**167**

Craig Warner—**173**

Stephanie Ye—**179**

Christopher Young—**183**

Sarah Young—**189**

ANJALI JOSEPH

Foreword

WHEN MY BROTHER WAS AROUND SIXTEEN A COUPLE OF HIS FRIENDS HAD A BABY. It wasn't exactly a planned pregnancy. One day my brother ran into the father in the supermarket. He was wheeling a pram containing a yowling infant. 'Want a baby?' he inquired sheepishly. 'It's fresh.'

Just after I graduated I lived in Paris for a year. My friends, like me, were anglophones who taught English, lived in tiny studios on top of tall buildings, and were excited about all that the city had to offer. Every year in France around the middle of November the new year's wine from Beaujolais would arrive, and as it did all the supermarkets and cafés bore signs that proclaimed this event: *Le Beaujolais nouveau est arrivé!* It was nice fruity red wine and we drank it chilled. Even better from the point of view of thrift, though, was the general *primeur*, red wine that wasn't much fermented and was halfway between grape juice and wine. It was sold near the exit of the supermarket and cost about three francs (at the time, 30p) for a litre and a half. It was kind of horrible. An Irish friend arrived at a house party with a bottle of *primeur* and announced, half-embarrassed, half-proud, 'The tramp outside my house had the same wine.'

Like any graduate of the UEA MA in Creative Writing, I have memories of the year of the course. The first few days, and the exaggerated first impressions we all made on each other. One of us had been a fighter pilot in Iraq. Someone else wore a pair of cufflinks made by American prisoners. One girl turned up with a bandage on her forehead and declared, pointing to her wound and

FOREWORD

then to a boy on the course, 'This is where he hit me last weekend.' I remember taking the bus to campus, the odd sense of theatre in and before a workshop, the peculiar damp, fetid, cigarettey smell of the upholstery in the Grad Bar, and a general sense of exhilaration and aspiration always undercut with fear and despair. I also remember going out to a bar with most of the other people on the course and at a certain point one evening having the strange realisation that, unlike other such evenings with different friends over the years, everyone else around the table was, like me, partially sitting back and watching the occasion unfold, and that this was what it could be like to socialise with other writers.

But why should you, the general reader, care about any of this? Partly there's the fun of guessing which of the writers in this anthology might go on to be published, what sort of thing they might write, if they'll be famous. Essentially this is gambling. But there's something else, too. Like the *primeur*, and maybe like the baby, what's contained between these covers may not be finished, polished, refined, aged, matured, or, always, made by someone who's certain of what she or he is doing. But because of all those things, what it does have is rawness, fizz, excitement, and probably a lot of highly stimulating enzymes. If you're lucky, it might even get you intoxicated quickly and inexpensively: in a word, it's fresh.

Anjali Joseph

JEAN McNEIL AND HENRY SUTTON

Introduction

IF THERE'S ONE WORD THAT BEST SUMS UP THE 2013/14 ACADEMIC YEAR, and its extraordinary cohort, it is optimism. Now, this is a word that doesn't often feature in creative writing or in literary circles more broadly. At the moment fiction publishing in the UK, as much as elsewhere, is undergoing great structural change – digitisation, the consolidation of larger publishing houses – yet it's also a time of great possibility and opportunity, thanks to the flourishing of smaller independent publishers and creative writing degrees like ours.

At UEA this year there has been a boom in literary readings, cabarets and events, many of them organised by our students. We also can't help noticing that there has been a marked increase in enthusiasm from all the industry professionals – agents and publishers alike – who have visited UEA this year, as well as a sense among the students that what they are doing really matters, that contemporary fiction, of whatever genre or literary register (as long as it's excellently conceived and executed), has a place in the culture, a future.

This optimism is no whistling in the dark, but part of a particularly complex, yet progressive understanding of the need for fiction, the writers of fiction, and the readers of fiction who expect to be challenged, informed and entertained in continually new and different ways, by new voices. Fiction has its roots in innovation. Even the word 'novel' attests to this. It can never be static, and would never aspire to be, which is why a course such as UEA's Prose Fiction MA is so intriguing. New writers appear

INTRODUCTION

on the course each year, increasingly from around the world. They bring with them vastly different experiences, resources, styles, techniques, intents and ambitions. The work collected here reflects the cosmopolitanism of our course, and the diverse subjects and locales our students approach in their work, from the dusty streets of Bahrain to gilded metropolitan soirées where the super-rich and an increasing army of zero-hours workers intersect. It is our pleasure to present a selection of the students' work in this annual anthology, which serves as a sampler to the diversity and achievement of their imaginations.

We write this as our course winds down for the year – a bittersweet moment for us all – yet we are increasingly aware that our students leave our course having had the benefit of an intensive year of experimentation, consolidation, reading, critiquing and dialogue. Their optimism often comes from the newfound certainty that they are not alone; that the networks and personal friendships established on our course will endure. For many of our students, no matter whether they scatter home to New Mexico or the Philippines, their peers from the UEA MA will continue to be their readers of first resort.

Jean McNeil
Henry Sutton
Joint Course Convenors, Prose MA

AYOBAMI ADEBAYO

Homecoming

HIS WIDOW DID NOT SEE HIM COME IN, BUT WE DID. He wore the same clothes he'd had on when he left for work about five weeks earlier, black suit, white shirt and a slim blue tie. He stood in the doorway for a moment, as though he expected her to look up, smile at him and apologise. She pulled at the ends of her headscarf and turned the page of the newspaper she was reading.

He shut the door and went into the sitting area without removing his shoes. Maybe he thought that would get her to talk to him. They'd argued so many times about the kind of shoes that could be worn on the cream rug that covered the floor. She placed the newspaper on her lap and rubbed her forearms the way she always did whenever she felt cold.

When he removed his jacket, we saw it: the massive blood stain that covered his back from shoulder blades to the point where his shirt disappeared into his trousers. The shirt clung to his back, obviously wet, as if five weeks later, the impact wound that had killed him was still bleeding.

He folded the jacket in two and put it on the arm of a black leather chair, the one he always sat in after they'd had a big fight. She'd never once abandoned the love seat they bought two months after they got married. He was always the one to get up in a huff and go to his black chair. We don't think he ever told her that it was a gift from Lope, his ex-girlfriend, the girl he'd once thought he'd marry.

He sat in the leather chair and stretched out his legs, waiting. For what? The truth is that throughout the ten months they were married, she was always the first to apologise. Their fights always ended the same way, with her on her knees in front of him, asking for forgiveness, even if he was the one who had been in the wrong. After she apologised, he would play with her hair and say he was sorry too. It was starting to bore us, their predictability. The couple that left before he moved in here four years ago was much more fun.

That night, he waited while she made her way slowly through the newspaper, reading every article the way she had done each night in the two weeks since her mother, his mother and all the other mourners left. Now and then he would clear his throat and give her a sidelong glance. He must have realised eventually that she was not going to get on her knees before him that night. So he did something he had never done before, he spoke to her before she apologised to him.

'I came home in a taxi,' he said to her. 'The driver was really nice, he didn't take any money from me. Imagine that in this Lagos. My car—' His voice dropped to a whisper. 'What happened to my car?'

While he shut his eyes and muttered softly about his car, she turned another page and moved closer to the centre of the newspaper, where his obituary lay next to an engine oil advert. He opened his eyes.

'Maria,' he said, jabbing a finger in her direction. 'About this morning. You need to learn to trust me. Yes, I was chatting with Lope last night, but you too shouldn't have snooped through my phone. You had no right.' He leaned back after he said this and glared at her.

She looked up briefly, in his direction, in the direction of the chair she'd told her mother she would always keep because it had been his favourite. When she shook her head slowly and returned her gaze to the newspaper, he sighed.

'OK,' he said. 'You had a right to. But, but, OK there is no but. You had every right to look through my phone. And since you did, you must have seen that I was just telling Lope how to move on. Look. Did the convo go on for too long? Maybe it did. But it's not as if I stayed up just to talk to her. You know I was studying for ACCA. That is why I was up. The convo with her was just on the side.'

She rubbed her eyes with the back of her right hand. Then she looked towards him, her lower lip held between her teeth, her eyes sorrowful.

'Look,' he said, leaning forward in his seat. 'I know you think I still have feelings for Lope, but Maria, I married you. You. Listen, after she sent that picture of her boobs last night, I stopped talking to her. You read the chats. You know I didn't say anything after that. And if you think I just deleted the things I said, why wouldn't I have deleted the picture too? Maybe I should have told her off when she sent the picture but I thought, I thought silence was better.'

He was telling her the truth. We had seen him shake his head and turn his phone face down on the glass-topped dining table after the picture came in. He'd gone back to his books after that and the phone had stayed that way until he went into the shower around five a.m. The next person to touch it was Maria. That was how their last fight started while he was still in the bathroom. It lasted through his shower, her shower. Their voices rose as they both dressed up. He dressed up quicker and stuffed the slim blue tie into his pocket instead of putting it on. She'd followed him to the door, her tailored shirt still unbuttoned, shouting questions he refused to answer. He'd slammed the door as he left and she'd leaned against one of us and sighed before stomping back into their room to finish dressing up for work.

Now, she sniffled as she turned another page and though she was not at the centre yet, even though she still had a couple of pages to go before the engine oil advert, tears were already trickling down her cheeks. He stood up and went to sit beside her in their grey loveseat. When he sat down, her body went still, and then it vibrated violently and went still again. She wiped her face with both hands and glanced at the spot where he sat to her right. She must have sensed his presence. Somehow, her body had sensed what her eyes could not perceive. They sat that way for a few moments, looking into each other's faces with only one seeing the other.

'I'm sorry,' he said. 'I'm sorry I hurt you.'

Maria reached out towards him. She let her right hand hover over his side of the loveseat, just a few inches above the knees she could not see. Then she pulled the hand back and put it over her heart. He touched the ends of the black scarf that covered her head, rubbed the fabric between his thumb and forefinger.

'Come on. Talk to me. Aren't you even surprised I said sorry first?' He pulled off the scarf, exposed her shorn head. 'What the—? Maria? Where's your hair?'

Maria did not shed a single tear as her hair was shaved off the day after it was confirmed that the body road traffic officers pulled out of the wreckage on third mainland bridge was her husband's. She sat with her back stiff and face dry as one of her sisters-in-law snipped away with a pair of scissors at her thick brown shoulder-length hair. It was Maria's mother who leaned against one of us, covered her face with both hands and wept. Sitting in the chair her husband had sat in while he chatted with Lope, Maria leafed through the textbooks he had neglected to put away in his hurry to get out of the house. Some of her hair fell on the pages. Her tears came later, after everyone – her mother, his mother, her sisters, his sisters, women who had come to comfort her and make sure she mourned the right way – went back home to their own husbands.

She was now on the obituary page of the newspaper. She lifted it as she always did when she got to this page, shifted to the left so she was closer to a light bulb, as though if enough rays shone on what she was reading, something would change, maybe the words, maybe the picture of the man she had married.

When she raised the newspaper, he stood up and leaned forward so he was looking directly into his own face. The picture had been taken at their traditional wedding. In it, he was decked in brown and gold. Two strings of coral beads hung around his neck, and his mouth was wide open, caught in the middle of a laugh. He shook his head as he stared at the page, at his funeral arrangements, at the list of friends who had signed their names in the bottom right corner.

'Maria,' he said. 'Maria, please stop this nonsense. You can hear me, Maria, you can hear me. I'm alive, Maria. I'm here.'

She covered the face in the newspaper with her palms, bowed her head and sobbed.

'Come on,' he yelled, backing away from her. He stood in the middle of the room, watching her weep, shaking his head over and over.

'I'm alive,' he said. 'I'm alive.'

And then, he came to one of us, the closest one to him. Perhaps he thought we would be the measure of what he had become. When he pressed his body against that wall and shut his eyes tightly, every one of us could feel him trying to breach us, trying to get through paint and concrete and steel to the other side. He did not break through, but somewhere in our foundations, we cracked. When he opened his eyes, he looked around and finding himself still in the living room and not in their bedroom, he smiled, went to Maria and knelt before her.

'Look,' he said. 'I'm here, I'm alive. You have to listen to me. Stop crying. Stop. Please.'

Then, he tried to hug her. But his arms disappeared into her body so that he was not holding Maria but had his hands stuck in her. When he pulled them out, she shrieked and cupped her shoulder, the points where his hands had been. His gaze moved back and forth between his hands and her tear- and snot-streaked face.

'No,' he said. 'No way.'

He tried again. This time he tried to hold her at the waist, but his hands got stuck inside her and when he managed to pull them out of her stomach she yelled, clutched her belly and doubled over.

'Oh God, I'm sorry,' he said, staring at his hands.

The newspaper had slipped from her lap when she doubled over. The pages were scattered on the floor around her feet. He turned them over one by one until he found the obituary. He traced his right thumb over every letter from 'Gone Too Soon' to the last 'Esquire' on the page. When he was done, he balled his hands into fists and howled. And the sounds they made, her sobs, his howl, became a single wave that shook the louvre blades.

Ayobami Adebayo was born in Lagos, Nigeria. Her work was highly commended in the 2009 Commonwealth Short Story competition. In 2012, she was a writer in residence at Writers Omi International (Ledig House), New York. In 2013, she was shortlisted for the Kwani? Manuscript prize for *Stay With Me*.

JOE BANFIELD

Romano Rai

An extract from a novella

BARNEY WALKED ROUND TO THE TRAILERS WITH ANOTHER BEER CAN IN HIS HAND. The sun was just dropping but the air still felt warm. A rough circle was marked out with traffic cones and some of the younger men, those that were fighting, limbered up and shadow-boxed to one side of it. Most of these were over from the Worthing camp. Two older men in shirts and jeans were working out the order of the fights, calling out to the gathering group and drawing names in chalk on a stone slab. Gildy Cooper sorted the money with Lloyd Dozzell.

Lloyd, who took all the bets, liked to hide the ante on top of his head, under a tweed flat cap. All the other bookies Barney had come across kept tabs in a notebook or a log, pencils lodged behind the ears, and counted the cash meticulously. But Lloyd had a unique way with money. He remembered everything. He took wagers seemingly without listening, glancing at the notes, stuffing them under his cap. Yet when the odds changed mid-fight he knew how much each man was in for, and what the bank was able to return. Gildy said Lloyd could hear money changing hands. He said that when Lloyd was a kid his father had sat him at the canasta table and made him deal the odds and spread the bets. Barney had been present at fairs and carnivals when Lloyd had guessed correctly how much change was in a jar. He measured out money like water. In his caravan he kept all the loose change he'd ever won in a five gallon container and he said that once it got to the top it would contain exactly eleven hundred pounds.

Barney pushed his way to the front of the crowd and took his place next to Ardan Halligan. There were a lot of faces he didn't recognise pressed in around him. People often came from other camps to see the fights. The crowd listed, shoaled, swaying like waves in the ocean, and a general quiet came over the whole site until two kids, both no older than sixteen, emerged into the open space and squared off.

Straight away, Lloyd was taking bets. Single pale arms rose into the air and waved notes or credit bills. Lloyd walked patiently round, inside the circle, gathering up the money and giving the odds. Barney never liked to place money before the fight started. Most times he could tell early, within the first few exchanges, who was going to win. He either knew then, straight up, or he never knew at all, and if he never knew he never speculated. This first fight he couldn't tell. It went slowly, both kids going for the jab-and-grab, throwing from range, then clinching. The crowd shouted at them to get on with it but the fight dragged and after a while, thirty minutes or so, one of the boys bent over exhausted, and waved it off. The referee, Jal Hanlon, held the other kid's arms up and the crowd, those that had won, started to line up in front of Lloyd, who was spraying the money out from his fingers like a hand-fan.

Barney stood next to Ardan Halligan. Two names were called out and a couple of boys Barney didn't know stripped out of their shirts and walked to the centre of the circle. Jal spoke to them both, gesturing with his hands, and they touched fists. One boy had a rat-tail and wore dark jeans, and the other was ginger-haired, close-shaved to the skull, and in a pair of jogging bottoms. They taped their hands and bumped fists then the fight began.

'They're both from the Worthing camp,' Ardan said. 'I've got thirty on the rat-tail.'

Barney could see why from the way Rat-tail moved. He was active, pressing the fight early on. He bobbed his head well, dipping from side to side, but Barney was unsure about his feet, which looked flat and heavy on the hard ground. Rat-tail shifted direction all in the torso and not the legs, and when he exchanged he came on in straight lines, giving the skinhead open angles to hit. The skinhead came out of a punch, rolling with the force in a kind of loose Philly Shell, and that's when Barney put Sabine's five on. The skinhead hadn't landed anything. He didn't even throw coming out of the exchange, but the way he drew Rat-tail on, offering out the shoulder, and then the way he moved laterally to free up punching space, told Barney the way the fight was going to go. Lloyd took the five at 4/5 which meant Barney stood to profit four pounds.

Ardan gave him a look and Barney said, 'Watch the feet. Your Rat-tail man tells you what he's going to do before he's done it. Too heavy-footed.'

Ardan looked back to Lloyd, then at the fight and said, 'Fuck.'

'Now you know,' Barney said.

Rat-tail came on again. He was small, a kid really, all forming muscle and unfinished body, yet he fought like a big man, slow in the legs, arms pitching heavily from side to side. The other kid, the skinhead, let Rat-tail duck and weave, and seemed content to wait, to let his opponent come on and come on until the punch was there and the fight could be won.

The small crowd started to get impatient again. Gildy Cooper wandered off. A man on the other side of the circle, possibly Rat-tail's father, was screaming at him to get inside and to smash the cunt out. Barney watched the feet. Skinhead was in football boots. He stepped in, feigned to put his weight on the leading leg, but then drew back out, letting Rat-tail fall into range. He hit him with a quick snap-jab and the crowd groaned.

'Thank God he didn't swing,' Ardan said.

Bartley Dozzell turned from the fight and said, 'Be all over if I had that shot. Hook, uppercut, anything but that.'

They closed in for a few wild exchanges, then Skinhead moved out of range again and waited, hopping from one foot to the other as if to convince himself and his opponent he wasn't as slow as he was. Both of them were bleeding from the nose. Barney finished his beer, crushed the can in one hand, and let it fall to the ground. Dogs on leashes barked. Barney could just hear them above the crowd. The punters screamed out for what they wanted their man to do. Ardan was quiet, but he threw little ghost jabs with every one of Rat-tail's punches, willing him on, teeth bared. Some of the children lurked between the trailers, trying to catch a glimpse of the fight, while others, those that were allowed, sat on their fathers' shoulders and looked down on the spectacle like little stone idols.

Rat-tail threw a wild right hand and the crowd roared. Skinhead bobbed, coming out head first, launching up with his own right. Rat-tail narrowly avoided it but the speed at which he was forced to move put him off balance. He stuck one hand on the ground and tried to spin away and around, in a kind of one-eighty, to keep himself front-on for the next punch. As he turned, Rat-tail brought his right hand, the one he'd had on the ground, swinging with the momentum of his body, in a wild arc. It was easy for Skinhead to stay inside this punch, to sit neatly inside the shadow of the slow-swinging arm, and get his feet planted. In the time it took the fist to come round, all the way from out wide, to meet him, Skinhead was already lining up his own shot.

'Game over,' Bartley said.

'Fuck,' Ardan said.

Skinhead hit him hard with his left hand. The crowd knew when to go quiet and the connection of fist on face cracked out of the trees and the earth beneath Barney's feet. The punch came from the shoulder, not the wrist, so it travelled all the way along the arm, picking up momentum as it went, like a tidal wave. When it landed the crowd made a kind of sucking-in noise. Barney kept his mouth shut and watched as Rat-tail went immediately horizontal. There was no mid-movement, no tumbling heavily down. One moment Rat-tail had been standing, throwing that clumsy, ungainly roundhouse, and the next he was reaching up off the ground, clawing on the air with both hands in an attempt to pull himself up, the eyes in his head like paper plates.

The crowd stayed for the next fight but Barney wanted to get back and check on Francie. He got his money from Lloyd, two copper coins and the returned five, and made his way back to the caravan. He'd wanted four pound coins so it felt like more money. Ten yards or so from the caravan the door opened and Gildy Cooper stepped out, coming down the mini-steps in his skin-tight red shorts, and closing the door behind him.

JOE BANFIELD

Barney was in his boots but they were still roughly the same height.

Gildy put his hands up and said, 'All right, Barney, I'm leaving.'

'You like sneaking round a man's home when he ain't there, Gildy?'

'Well, it ain't technically your home, is it?'

'Technically it ain't yours neither.'

'Hey. I saw Sabine was in and wanted to see how the little man was.'

'I told you how he was earlier. If you wanted to see him you shoulda come to the hospital yesterday.'

'All right. Well, I'm leaving now, anyhow.'

'It's what Da woulda done, when he was rom baro.'

Gildy looked past Barney, to show he wanted to get round him, but Barney wasn't moving.

'You want me to explain the rules, Gild? You the rom baro and all. A man's home is his castle,' Barney said.

Gildy smiled.

'You got that?'

The smile slowly went and Gildy said, 'Barney, I think you and I are gonna have a big falling out one day.'

Barney went inside. He looked out the door before he closed it. Gildy was hobbling away, back to the trailers. Sabine stood with her back to him, both hands on the table. Her apron lay in a heap on the floor and there were steady drips of water falling on it from the sideboard. Barney went into the bedroom. Francie and Queenie were playing with some toy cars on their bed. They looked up as he entered, curious.

'Gildy been to see you?' Barney said.

Francie nodded slowly, dumbly.

Barney closed the door. Back in the main interior, Sabine turned round. She took a deep breath and smiled hopefully, smoothing herself down with both hands. Barney approached. He drew out the five pound note and gave it back to her. She waited, leaning against the table. Barney angled his head to one side and gave her a look. Then he took a small step back, his boots scuffing the carpet a little. She tried a smile. He took his watch off, placed it carefully on the side, turned back to Sabine, lined her up, and lashed her hard across the face with the back of his hand.

Joe Banfield was born in Brighton. He graduated from UEA in 2013, having studied English Literature and Creative Writing. He is currently working on a second draft of a novella about gypsy bare-knuckle boxing, set in modern-day Brighton.

JULIA BREENS

The Bitter Red

Chapter one of a novel

EVERYTHING IS READY FOR HIS ARRIVAL, THE MAN FROM *THE NEW YORK TIMES*. There's a new cloth on the patio table around the back and I bought cushions for the hard seats. I even ironed my blouse, which is pristinely white, although I'm wearing jeans and not something smart like a skirt because I want to feel comfortable during the interview.

What will he think of this place? This huge house in its cage of towering beeches and sweet chestnuts, the air ripe with the smell of overgrown vegetation. If I compare it to some of the mansions Saskia and I stayed at on our grand tour then it's little more than a doll's house, but it's bigger than the place I grew up in, more than twice the size. He will ask me where I got the money, I realise. And I don't know what I'll say.

Standing in the front garden, on a threadbare patch of grass that isn't worthy of the title 'lawn', I've found the one puddle of sunlight that's managed to break through the crowd of trees. Between the trunks I can see fragments of the road a quarter of a mile to the east of the property and I wait, listening to the whistle and coo of the birds high above me.

I find I'm nervous for the first time in years and while I'm used to being scared, nerves are different. Nervousness is a reaction to a threat that won't physically harm you. Being scared is what happens when you fear for your life. I'm worried about the questions the journalist will ask, whether I will answer them with confidence. Be strong, Ash told me on the phone a few hours ago, show him you're unbroken. But I am broken, Ash.

THE BITTER RED

I pat my pocket to make sure my pack of Camels is there. Of course it hasn't gone wandering, no sticky fingers other than mine to take it wandering, but this is instinctive behaviour now, with me until the end.

A glint of silver to the south of the house catches my eye and I hold my breath. The glint moves from left to right, twinkling in the gaps between the trees. It's definitely a car, but it's not turning off onto the rutted track leading to the house. It's continuing towards Fontenay. False alarm. Stand down.

My patch of sun is stolen by a cloud. I wait for it to return. Sometimes I hate Ash for choosing this place. The most remote he could find, he'd said, without being a hundred-year-old shack with an outside toilet and no running water, but I would have been OK with a shack, as long as it received its fair share of light, because it's the gloominess that I can't stand.

Until late afternoon, the sun has its work cut out trying to penetrate the foliage. On very fine days, it manages to break through in a rash of bright spots that shift around on the grey brick. Once the sun swings round to the west, about five o'clock at this time of year, it pries its way through a wedge of space between the trees and the wide frontage of the house is lit up in shades of amber and coral for half an hour or so. It's lovely then, but it isn't enough. Sometimes I drive to the nearest town and sit in the square, basking like a lizard on a bench by the fountain, my skin pinkening and growing hot, and yet in the car on the way back I can always feel the gloom latched tightly about my shoulders. It's become part of me somehow.

The patch of blue hydrangeas in the border next to me is swaying in the breeze, the blooms bulbous and grotesque. I didn't like them when I arrived. I thought about digging them up, but they're everywhere in France, outside supermarkets, by the side of the roads, so I suppose I just got used to them. When the wind ripples through them they bob around on their stubby stalks as though they're gossiping with each other. I hope it's good gossip today. Quality gossip. Something to scandalise the hydrangea community. I wonder if they're talking about me. I like to think so.

Another glimmer catches my eye, a fleck of red in the distance.

Another car. This one isn't passing by. It has already turned onto the track and is winding its way up to the house, so I walk over to the semicircle of dirt where my eleven-year-old Citroen is parked and where he will have to pull up.

There are three shallow bends in the track and when I next see the vehicle through the foliage he's rounding the last of these. He's close enough that I should be able to see him, but the interior of the car is dark compared to the bright September afternoon and I'm on full view, so I raise my hand in greeting.

The car rolls slowly onto the dirt drive and stops. It's a Megane. French plates. A rental car. He's little more than a shadow inside, further obscured by slats of sunlight that bounce off the windscreen, but I can see some movement. He's ferreting around with things on the passenger seat, making me wait.

The door cracks open, the sound of the seals releasing from each other, and he reveals himself to me in pieces. A foot. A hand curled around the edge of the door. A shin and a knee. The rest of him all at once. A pleasant shape, broad shoulders, slim hips, all wrapped in jeans and a white shirt. Now this is embarrassing. We've turned up to the ball in the same gown.

He's wearing a pair of aviators, which he removes as he steps towards me, and he's smiling, broadly though not necessarily convincingly. I'm not surprised to see that he is handsome. Looks must be an advantage in his line of work; people open up to an attractive stranger more easily than an ugly one, a truth I learned a long time ago. It's not an interesting kind of handsome though. There's nothing about the angles of his face, the high sweep of cheekbones or the set of his jaw that speaks of uniqueness, and while I've always found that a good pair of eyes – a flash of hazel under hooded lids, for instance – can be the hinge upon which a face succeeds or fails, his are too pretty, the colour of bluebells in spring, and they're at odds with the rest of his features. They belong in another face.

I hold out my hand and we shake.

'Charlie McCartey. Thanks for inviting me to your home, Miss Lowell.'

So formal and professional.

'Adele, please. How was your journey?'

THE BITTER RED

I can still put on a show of normal human behaviour, but I'm not actually interested in his answer, so I watch his mouth move as he talks about delays at JFK and queues at the Hertz at La Rochelle. His American accent is all East Coast; he's aiming for Long Island Lockjaw, I think, trying to inject a touch of old-fashioned class and status into his voice, but it's mashing against some Boston and a touch of Brooklyn. If there's something to be said for a stretch in a US prison, it's that the jumpsuits focus one's attention on the people inside them, their mannerisms, the way they talk, and I always had a talent for accents to begin with. I would mimic people after hearing them speak only a couple of sentences. It became my party trick, Saskia insisting I perform at every gathering we hosted or attended, usually for men she fancied or wanted something from.

'Dan's from Louisville, Addie, show him your Kentucky.' Or 'Zach's grandmother was Minnesota born and raised'. And I'd have to respond with 'Hey, ya guys, ya know d'eres a leak in the ruf'. And everybody would find it hysterical that it was coming out of the mouth of an English girl.

'I thought we'd sit on the terrace out back, if that suits you?' I say to my visitor.

'Fine, fine.' His gaze flits around, taking in the house, my car, up to the tops of the tall trees that are gently rustling all around us, briefly to me again, my face, my body, not lingering anywhere. Some people are easy to read. He is not one of them, though I detect perhaps the hint of a frown across his brow. Is he disappointed? Was he expecting me to look as I did back then? There was one image in particular of my arrest, in which I was being bundled into a police car, and that I later discovered was reprinted in almost every news article about me until the trial ended. I remember the moment it was taken, amid the confusion and chaos, hearing someone calling my name and looking up to be greeted by a piercing light. In the photo, I am wide-eyed, my skin bleached by the flash, though I must have had a healthy tan at the time, and my face is framed by the glossy dark hair that I thought suited me so well.

I no longer dye my hair, which is now its natural mousy nothingness and liberally streaked with white. These green eyes, my best feature as I was forever being told, are crowded out by wrinkles. I'm only forty-two, but it would be difficult to recognise me as the woman in that image and perhaps that's why he frowns.

He goes back to the car to fetch his bag before I lead him carefully up the steps – five big concrete slabs gone crooked where the earth has subsided beneath them over the years – and tell him to go round the side of the house to the terrace while I make tea in the kitchen.

On the tray, I place the china pot, cups and saucers – covered in hand-painted irises – that Nana left to me in her will and which Ash delivered to me in my first week here.

'A little taste of home, sweetheart,' he'd said as I carefully unfurled the tissue paper it was wrapped in. When he left I cried, because it wasn't a little taste of home; it was all that was left of home. Home was stripped down and sold after Nana's death while I was in a cell an ocean away.

Carrying the tray out to the terrace I find that Charlie McCartey has already settled into a chair, leaving me the bench on the other side of the table. He stands up and offers to take the tray, which is good manners wasted in an entirely futile gesture, because I've managed to bring it all the way from the kitchen and it's only three feet to the table. So I tell him it's fine and to sit down, which he does, immediately. There it is, I decide. The first sign that he's frightened of me.

Julia Breens was born in Leicester and now lives in Warwickshire. She is passionate about crime fiction and is in the process of writing *The Bitter Red*, a thriller about lives that are ruined in the fallout of a friendship gone sour.

MARK CHAIKEN

Now

An extract

THE DOOR TO THE NURSES' ROOM IS OPEN. There are always some Nurses in their room.

Mrs Fox is here now. I see that Aya is already here too, curled up in Mrs Fox's lap, even though she's almost as big as Mrs Fox, so really only the top half of her will fit and her legs hang down over the side of the big white chair where Mrs Fox is sitting. Mrs Fox is stroking Aya's black hair. Her hand seems so small and pale against all that black. Mrs Fox looks sad, but I cannot see Aya's face, as she is turned away. Mrs Fox looks up at me for just a moment, then looks down at Aya's face, which I cannot see, and starts stroking her hair again.

Mrs Wolf is sitting on one of the couches and I go over to her, half-sitting so that my face is pressed against her chest and my legs aren't hanging down like Aya's, but they're partly in Mrs Wolf's lap and partly on the cushions. Mrs Wolf is big, with thick legs and thick arms and a chest that sticks out in front of her, and she has grey hair that won't stay underneath her white cap. Strands of it escape and float across her ears and her eyes so that she pushes them back and tries to force them to stay under her cap again. She has big green eyes that can see me when they're not looking at me. All the other Nurses do what she tells them to do.

The stiff white fabric of her uniform is rough against my cheek, and it feels good so I rub my face softly up and down against her. She smells like my sheets, clean and white, and this time I don't resist my instincts, I let it all wash over me,

NOW

the feeling of safety, when all the information is all right to know.

Mrs Wolf's hand is on the back of my head, heavy and comforting, but I hear her say, 'Too close.'

I pull my face away from her chest and look up at her. She is not looking at me, she is looking at Mrs Fox, and at Aya in her lap.

She feels my change in position and looks down at me now. With her arm she sits me straight up. She doesn't force me. She doesn't grip me hard. Her hand firmly suggests the position that she wants my body to attain, and my body obeys.

She stares at me with her big green eyes, but she is careful not to meet my gaze directly for too long, not with our faces so close together, and she looks away when she speaks.

'Now what is the matter, dear?'

I press my face against Mrs Wolf's chest. She consents to stroke my hair, but only briefly before she pushes me back again.

'What is wrong with Aya?'

'There's nothing to worry about, dear. She just had a bad dream. Is that what happened to you? Did you have a bad dream?'

From the way she asks me this question, I think she wants me to say yes. I see Mrs Fox is still stroking Aya's hair, but she's looking at me as though she's interested in my answer too.

I do not like to disappoint Mrs Wolf, so it is hard for me to speak at first. 'No. I have a piece of paper.'

Mrs Wolf does not seem upset by this answer, so I am happy and continue.

'There are words on the paper.'

Mrs Swan freezes and lets out a little piping sound. I forget she is there except when she stops moving. Mrs Wolf looks at her and raises one eyebrow. 'Paper very often has words on it,' she says, as much to Mrs Swan as to me. 'I don't think we should make too much of this.'

I force my head forward, halfway back to Mrs Wolf. Not enough to hide my words completely, but maybe enough so that the words are trapped between us, in the narrow space between our two bodies. 'I read the words.'

Mrs Wolf's hand stops moving and instead it just lies on the back of my head. But it feels so heavy that my head is forced down against her chest, and I wonder if she means to silence me completely, to suffocate me for what I have said. Her chest heaves, up, down, up again, and then she releases me to breathe, pressing the side of my face instead to herself. Her hand resumes its rhythm over my hair. I succumb.

'The words go away,' I say, hoping to redeem the disappointment I know she feels.

More gently, Mrs Wolf lifts me off her lap and stands up. She takes my hand and pulls me up to stand too. 'Well, I think we should at least investigate the situation,' she says as she starts to walk towards the door. She is holding my hand and I walk beside her. She releases it and takes my shoulders to propel me through the door ahead of her. I turn at her touch. From the corner of my eye I see Mrs Fox looking down at Aya; and I see Aya, her head turned towards me now, tears in her eyes, but smiling.

'Be careful how you phrase it,' says Dr Mason. 'An enormous amount of information can be conveyed in even very simple questions. Keep it vague.'

Mrs Fox gives him a strange look that involves her turning her head away from him to stare at Mrs Wolf. But I can still tell somehow that the look is directed towards him. Mrs Wolf does not say anything. She does not change her face. She takes something from the metal tray behind her and sits down.

'Can you tell me what this is?' Mrs Wolf is sitting across from me on a low stool. It is much shorter than she is, and her knees are sticking out in front of her, out from under her stiff white skirt. Her knees are covered in thin white fabric that clings to her skin, and I can see that she has big round knees, pressed together like friends. She is holding a card almost two-thirds of a metre from my face. There is a slight tremor in her hand, though maybe that is caused by the breeze from the ventilator high up on the wall. I can feel the air stirring the hairs on the top of my head. I want to raise my hand to smooth them down. I don't like the sensation of the air moving across them, disordering them. It feels like someone invisible is standing behind me, breathing down on me.

NOW

There is no one standing behind me. Mrs Wolf is sitting in front of me, holding the card up. Mrs Wolf is asking me a question. The card is a question.

On the card are printed thick black lines. My sight tells me that the lines are thick and distinct against the white background, but still I can only see them as blurred, as though my mind refuses to focus as sharply as my eyes.

I think Mrs Wolf is asking me something about the black lines on the card. Should I tell her what they look like to me? Should I tell her what my eyes see or what my mind sees? Mrs Wolf and Mrs Fox and Dr Mason are all staring at me so hard that my skin begins to itch.

'It is a card with black lines on it.'

Dr Mason leans back. The muscles in his face relax so that he is almost smiling. But Mrs Wolf is still looking at me like she's expecting me to continue, and I see that Mrs Fox is opening her mouth as though she's saying something, though no sound is coming out. And then it seems to me that she is not saying something, she actually is making a sound, just one sound, even though I still cannot hear anything, and I hear her making that sound in this room, right now, but not now. There is sound and there is no sound.

Mrs Fox's mouth is closed again, and there is no sound.

The lines snap into focus. 'They make the letter "A".'

Dr Mason jumps when I say that, and I can smell the sweat I see beading on his forehead. But when Mrs Fox looks at me her eyes are slightly creased up at the corners.

'Yes, the letter "A". How do you know that?' asks Mrs Wolf. She alone is showing no reaction, and there is no change in the tone of her voice. I think that my answer does not surprise her, and that she knows the answer to this second question she is asking.

'You teach me.' I do not know if these words are true. Mrs Wolf doesn't say anything, still doesn't show any reaction, just nods her head.

'When did I teach that to you?'

'Now.'

She is silent for a moment. 'Good,' she says, and stands up to join the other two. Her knees crack as she rises.

'I knew we shouldn't even have asked. It's always better to leave well enough alone and remain ignorant.' Dr Mason hisses at Mrs Wolf and Mrs Fox, angry and scared and not afraid to show it. I understand. I am not supposed to know the letter "A".

'What's done is done,' says Mrs Wolf. 'In any event, the information doesn't appear to have led to breakdown. Since we've started down this road, we need to continue. There may be important answers here.'

I wonder if I should tell them that I know the other twenty-five letters too, upper and lower case. And little a as well. I wonder if there are some letters I don't know, whether there are some letters so upsetting that I can't even be told they exist. I don't say anything.

'Are you insane?' Dr Mason is trying to keep his voice down, as though he thinks by speaking softly he can pretend I am not there. Perhaps I am not there if he pretends I am not there. Perhaps I only remember being there. 'That's completely outside of protocol! Think of the damage you could do. Contamination on that level could compromise the entire programme. We can contain a single letter, but actual reading? Do you want them all to freeze?'

'As I said, Dr Mason, what's done is done. This decision has clearly already been made. Though, of course, I have no more memory of teaching her than she has of learning. But you understand how these things happen. Now, if you please, I have work to do.'

Mrs Wolf turns to lift another card from the metal tray, but she doesn't show it to me yet. Dr Mason is standing perfectly still, refusing to accept dismissal. They look at each other for ten seconds exactly, neither moving.

'Dr Smith and Dr Miller will hear about this!' Dr Mason sputters at last, and almost runs from the room.

Mrs Wolf turns back to me, still not revealing the card. Mrs Fox is standing behind her, red-brown eyes that have been smiling silently the whole time now relaxing into calm observation. Mrs Wolf blinks at me, but Mrs Fox does not.

NOW

'The letter "X",' I say.
It will be.

Mark Chaiken grew up in New York and London. He spent ten years studying philosophy of time, though it felt like fewer. He has completed one book, *Blank*, a satire about a creator's responsibilities to his creations, and is working on a second, *Now*, about the phenomenology of time travel.

DAVE CHUA

The Ditch

WHEN SHE WAKES SHE FINDS HERSELF STRAPPED IN THE BACK SEAT OF A JEEP. Her mouth is gagged with a small towel from the hotel and she can only sputter. Hands zip-tied, the seat belt crosses her body like a beauty pageant sash.

The driver grunts. She can't make out his features except that his face is pockmarked. Another man, in a leather jacket, on the left passenger seat, turns back and smiles, as if trying to reassure her. There is a container on the passenger's lap; he looks like he is going on a picnic. Driver mutters something about using more chloroform. Passenger asks her if she is hungry.

She tries to reply but can't say anything. She wonders if he is mocking her. She wants lamb stew cooked for hours, until the meat pulls away from the bone like candy floss. Still drowsy, the lights of the cars they pass are as faraway as stars.

She has seen Passenger before. He was with his boss in Paris, always hovering in the background.

She tries to stay awake. She holds on to the memory of her arms circling around her husband, while they speed on a motorcycle through cracked roads, honking at lambs. Recognising the futility of begging, she hums, through the towel, a lullaby to her children. She thinks of her daughters, probably sound asleep in their father's house. They have outgrown the mattress she bought, their legs dragging on the cold concrete floor. She only calls late at night because she does not want them to hear her. The oldest will already be able to judge her for fleeing them and the country.

THE DITCH

She tries to think of what she can say. Her breathing is so heavy it fills the jeep.
Have you dived? Driver asks Passenger, countering the silence.
No. I don't swim. Almost drowned when young, Passenger replies.
You should. Our country has some of the best diving. Sidapan, Tioman. Water clear like glass.
I can't learn to swim now.
When you're down there, you're surrounded by this blueness, and all the coral. It's amazing, *abang*. I was diving two weeks ago, and there was this school of barracuda. You know how they swarm around, and when you first see them, all you remember are their teeth.
They don't bite you?
They won't. Humans don't taste good to them. They're after fish. They just circle around us. It's like you are caught in a disco ball. Hypnotised.

All she can do is watch the traffic outside the jeep; the low boom of sound as they pass cars and lorries.
She remembers that at this time of the year, the weather in her country would be starting to cool, days of high blue skies and the horizon a single unbroken line.
They turn onto a highway, pass some half-hearted barriers. Driver squeezes the jeep past them, the vehicle rocks back and forth, its wheels tossing up gravel. Passenger complains about the suspension; it feels like he is on a massage chair gone amok. Knowing that they are nearing their destination, she tries to scream but ends up choking on the fibres. She tries to struggle and free herself, slamming her body against the seat but the two just ignore her.

The highway is unlit. The jeep is the only vehicle on the smooth, freshly paved road. Driver presses down on the accelerator until Passenger cautions him to slow down. They are driving on the country's future, on a newly-birthed road that hugs the low hills. They are not far away from the city and they can still see lights spilling into the night sky.

She knows that they carry guns. Desperately, she tries to come up with something that can change her fate. Passenger's fingers tap the basket. She wonders if she will even have a chance to speak.

The jeep takes a turn, diving right into the jungle. It stops at a clearing, abandoned and empty. There is a maze of ditches around them.

Meant to be a rest stop, but they got more money so moved it further down, Driver says.

Who would want to have a rest stop here?

Not about the stop. About the contracts.

The boss in this?

He has a finger in everything. He's like a dam. It all flows to him, right?

They take her from the back seat and her feet drag in the mud. Driver pushes her into a ditch. Her head strikes the soggy earth. She lies there, wondering if they are going to leave her there. Maybe that's all they will do.

Driver jumps into the ditch and turns her to face him. She can hardly make out his features. He removes the towel from her mouth. She asks for mercy; she tells them about the child inside her, in English, Russian, French, Malay and even Mongolian. She says she will return to her country and never disturb their boss again.

Driver apologises, and says that it is because of the child inside her that they have to do this. He raises the gun, allowing her time to pray.

She tries to keep a memory, knowing it might be her last. She tries to remember singing lullabies to her first daughter, but the one memory that sticks is that of being in the Paris subway one evening, alone, fearful. The tunnel is dark and she stares at the billboards advertising vodka and trips to Taiwan. When the train finally arrives, she is so relieved that she feels a joy so clear it bursts her heart. The scene of the train crawling to the station is trapped in her head. She curses herself for the memory clamped to her brain.

In the ditch, her body folded, she resembles a baby on the verge of being released from the womb. Driver drags himself out of the ditch, brushing away the soil, putting away his gun.

THE DITCH

Your turn, he says to Passenger.

After putting on his gloves, Passenger opens the container and takes out the C4. He steps carefully into the ditch. Trying to figure out the best way to place the explosives on her body is like a puzzle. When the headlights go off, he is terrified. Driver turns them back on, laughing at Passenger's fear. After his hands have calmed down, Passenger places the explosives around her. Her eyes refuse to shut; they flick open every time he closes them. The blood seeping into the ground is like tar. His sweat drips onto the soil; it has been years since he has set explosives.

Driver complains about not getting a cell phone signal and Passenger scolds him; he is trying to concentrate. Satisfied that the explosives are in place, Passenger scurries out like a desperate mole. They back the jeep away. But when Passenger presses the button on the detonator, the explosives do not go off. The jungle fires back accusations. Monkeys chatter. They edge the jeep nearer, and Passenger keeps punching the button but nothing happens. Driver lets out a half-sigh.

Passenger returns to the ditch, sweating like he's just run a marathon. Driver complains that he is missing soccer. He turns on the radio, but only gets white noise.

Driver asks Passenger if he knows the right phrase to say to the tree spirits before he takes a pee, and Passenger tells him just to apologise to them. Driver asks if he can take a shit, and Passenger tells him to just hold it in.

They still hear lorries grumbling on the road far off.

We are not far enough, says Passenger.

Scared or what? The employer will protect us, says Driver.

Driver and Passenger know each other from their terms as police officers before becoming bodyguards. The pay is far better, they get to travel the world and they do not have to listen to ridiculous complaints, although Driver sometimes misses the days when he could get into fist fights, swinging his baton and smashing heads. He knew how to incite someone into attacking, which expletives to use.

Passenger remembers when Boss first met the girl. She was translating for some businessman with a bushy moustache, and Boss kept staring at her and nodding. He wanted to warn her to stay away, to turn down the boss's dinner invitation, but he always knew how to keep his mouth shut. He wonders now if he can just turn back, saying that the explosives are faulty, have her body returned to her country, but it is now all too late.

Once he rearms the explosives, they back away. Passenger presses a button to set off the charge, pumping it furiously, but once again the bomb does not go off. Driver passes him a cigarette. He turns off the headlights of the jeep and they are once again in darkness. The trees above form veins of sky.

Just relax, *abang*, Driver says. He massages Passenger's shoulders. They take in the quiet of the jungle. After they finish their cigarettes, the headlights come on again and Passenger tries once more.

Driver asks for some of the C4 to smoke. He heard from an American he met in Copenhagen that they can give a high. Passenger tells him to go off and smoke his cigarettes and not to disturb him.

Bored, Driver goes to sleep while Passenger works on the explosive. He has placed the bath towel over her face. He hears Driver slapping mosquitos.

The problem is with the explosives. Who knows how long they were kept before they were passed to him? He shapes it over her body, as if he is making a mould, presses the wires deeper. Even now, her skin is still warm. He picks off an earthworm that crawls across her cheek, refusing to let them mar her pale skin.

After about thirty minutes, he wakes Driver up and they reverse the jeep. Driver asks to push the detonator. Passenger hands it to him.

Good luck, Passenger says.

The explosion sounds like Chinese firecrackers popping, and a burst of birds scatter into the sky. The whole jungle is awakened by the noise. Earth rains down on them and the jeep. Driver lets out a whoop of triumph.

He gives Passenger a thumbs up. There is a crater large enough to swallow a house. Passenger wants some petrol to burn the remains but Driver says it is too complicated to drain any from the tank. They leave her masticated body for the jungle to consume.

THE DITCH

Isn't this how the corpses are dealt with in their country? Their bodies broken into pieces? says Driver, on the drive back.
No, I think that's Nepal. Or Tibet.
Passenger thinks he can hear the explosion still echoing amongst the trees. Driver drops Passenger off at his house; dawn is creeping into the sky. As Passenger fumbles for his house keys, he still sees light scrawls in his eyes, the explosion burned into his corneas.

When the sun emerges, the Native spots the tyre tracks leading from the road. He imagines partygoers, fuelled on alcohol and ganja, partying through the night, and hopes to retrieve some leftover beer bottles. The city people always forget about those who still dwell in the forest.
The tracks of the jeep lead to a single large crater, where a fierce light beckons him. At the edge of the crater he finds an earring, small as a dot, reflecting the sun. After he pockets it, he notices the shattered body, the human remnants scattered amongst the new mud, the broken earth.

Dave Chua has published a novel entitled *Gone Case* and his collection of short stories, *The Beating and Other Stories*, was longlisted for the 2012 Frank O'Connor International Short Story prize.

KRISHAN COUPLAND

Friends

A short story

IT WAS INCREDIBLE, REALLY, THE WAY HE LOST EVERYTHING – that the plane which carried Fin's mother and father should fall with such precision onto the car that contained his wife and child. Fin could not believe it at first, when the policeman came for him at work. Yes, he said, he would like to see the bodies. He sat there in the back of the police car, still calm as a tightrope walker, as an electrified rail. Nothing was real. Not the policemen nor the hospital nor the cool efficiency of the mortuary. Even the bodies were elaborate fakes, dressed dolls made up in shades of blue. Actors, perhaps, lying there barely containing their laughter at this wonderful prank they were playing on him – wonderful for its sheer scale, for the taking out and bringing home again of his soul... except there was no bringing home, there was no end to it, and the bodies never lifted themselves smiling from those metal racks, never rose warm into him again like returning birds, and he was alone and alone and alone.

After the funerals Fin lay on the sofa and watched TV. He watched *Friends*, and when he was lonely he would talk to them. To Joey and Phoebe and Chandler, lost in the petty dramas of their lives, so comfortable and safe that he felt drugged. *Oh no, Joey and Chandler lost the baby. Oh no, Ross said Rachel's name at the wedding.* He dozed there for months, for lifetimes, skin drying in his dressing gown like some shallow terrycloth cocoon. He marked time only by the impulses of his body: ate when hungry, drank when thirsty, pissed when he needed to piss. It was bleak, endless. But *Oh no, Rachel told Joey her boss wants to buy her baby.*

FRIENDS

The utter happiness of it, that he had known, that he himself had known some time ago – it made him feel as if something were pushing at the inside of his chest, trying to escape. He put his hands there, against the tufted towelling of his gown and held it back, held it behind his ribs.

Mail accrued on the doormat, and sometimes Fin would go to the slew of papers and stir them with his foot, but nothing more. Sometimes the phone would ring, and Fin would wait for it to stop. Once, it didn't stop, and Fin counted fifty, then a hundred, then two hundred rings before he went to it and ripped the cord from the wall. After that nobody called again. He hauled the heavy dresser from the front room and wedged it against the door. He kept the curtains shut, turned the TV up loud to drown out any sounds from the street. In the dark the screen threw out light and Fin couldn't tell where that world ended and this world began. He fell asleep in front of it, and in his dreams he was safe and unburdened, and the things that afflicted him were small, funny, bearable things. A sick duck. A missing lunch. A chair he could never possibly afford. The screen was the first thing he would see when he woke, and to his sleep-softened brain it seemed unbearably real.

Fin didn't go upstairs. Upstairs was the past. Upstairs was a memorial or a museum exhibit, old bones held together by wire. Upstairs was where the grief lurked like a mugger, ready to come running from the shadows and shuttle itself into his chest. If he went upstairs he would cry again, he knew it. Fin hated to cry, being inside the sound of it like a man in a failing submarine. That animal whine extruding from himself, pathetic and lonely as childhood. But what could he do? Keep a watch? Sit up at night to make sure those old bones didn't come creeping down to touch him while he slept? In the end he hauled the bookcase from the front room and toppled it awkwardly against the steps, as much a barrier as he could manage.

A month after that, in the middle of the night, Fin woke to silence. Everything was dark, and that itself struck him like a snakebite. He sat up. The TV was blank, the room cold enough for his breath to make vapour. When he tried it the light switch did nothing and, cold, he returned to the sofa and his duvet. He tried not to think. He could hear the grief moving around upstairs, pawing through drawers, trying on his clothes, admiring itself in the mirror. He got up and wrapped his coverings around him like a cloak and went to the foot of the stairs. The quiet was awful, pressing on his eardrums, occlusive and dark. He wondered what the Friends were doing right now. What it was that he was missing. He went to the cupboard under the stairs and felt out the box of trip switches and clicked them this way and that to no result. He felt faintly sick. What would Chandler do if he were here? He paced for a while, to help keep warm, then went and lay again on the sofa. The rest of that night he did not sleep.

They came for him soon after that. Fin heard them knocking on the door, shouting his name through the letterbox, and he went out into the hall. He could see them over the top of the dresser, their faint shapes made angular by frosted glass. Two women dressed in blue. They were shouting his name, but he didn't reply. *We know you can hear us*, they said, and then they started hitting the door, hard, and Fin was afraid. *We're worried about you. Lots of people are worried about you.* Fin went upstairs, scrabbling up over the smooth back of the bookshelf. He wasn't scared anymore. Not now that it was quiet. Not now that they were coming for him. He went to his daughter's room and sat on her bed and took her soft toys, her lions and cats and bears and seals and held them and tried to find some scent of her on them. He took them and went to the room he and his wife had shared. He lay on the bed. The room was musty, damp-smelling. There was no grief waiting for him behind the door. He barely remembered, anymore, the exact shape of her face. He turned over the photographs beside the bed, and hugged the soft toys and waited.

Downstairs they were shouting through the letterbox again. *You can't stay in there forever*, they yelled.

Fin shut his eyes. *Yes*, he thought, *I can.*

Krishan Coupland lives in Norwich. His short fiction and poetry have appeared in *Brittle Star, Aesthetica, Ambit* and *Fractured West*. He won the Manchester Fiction Prize in 2011, and in his spare time he edits a literary magazine. More of his work can be found via www.krishancoupland.co.uk.

ALICE FALCONER

A Geometry of Ghosts

Extract from a novel

'**WHAT'RE YOU LOOKING AT NOW?**' **RAY SAYS.** He has stopped washing up, and in the quiet I can hear a bird calling somewhere outside the boat. I'm looking at one of the portholes, set low in the cabin wall. The glass seems to be quartered by silvery lines that cross in the centre, scattered with velvet-black dots each about the size of a penny. I bring my face closer. The back of my neck hurts from craning. The bird calls again, two-tone like a swinging gate, and the dots tremble, cluster together and push into each other to build a moorhen, solid and squawking, paddling outside the porthole. It feels my stare and cracks its beak wide to hiss; the inside is a surprisingly human pink. I step back. The glass is clear again.

'What *is* it?' Ray asks, panicky, but irritated too; he doesn't like not knowing straight away. With a snap he pulls off each marigold glove, ready to hug, or squeeze, an answer out of me.

He wouldn't like to know that my so-called visions consist of points and crosses, lines and squares. When they began I confused them with the floaters that occasionally drift through anyone's sight. Then they got sharper, brighter, more frequent. They seem benign. But they're not what Ray hopes for, or fears. Ghouls aren't geometric.

'Not a ghost this time,' I say. 'Don't worry.'

He tugs at his collar, nervously. As if I've just read his mind, when it's so obvious, his skull could be made of glass. I touch his sleeve, smile at him. 'Kath'll be at the bus stop soon. Should you go get her?'

'Your wish is my command,' he says, putting on a strange voice to show that it is not, even as he reaches for his jacket.

'I'll get ready,' I say.

Once he's gone I just sit, till it's dark outside. I like being alone in his boat. If I loosed the blue nylon hawsers it would slip downriver like a seal, through the marshes and out of London, into the Grand Union Canal. The boat tugs at its moorings as though it has come to a decision.

But he'll be back soon, with this woman, Kath. The bus will let her out on the main road that crosses the marshes. No houses on that stretch, just scrappy trees and fields behind. Unlikely to be anyone else at the bus stop, just an advert for MIND so old it's slipped down behind the glass and crinkled into a concertinaed pile. Londoners aren't used to darkness – real darkness, not just the dirtiness of the orange sky at four a.m. or the gloom between each puddle of streetlight. She'll be rattled, nervous. Then Ray comes out of the gloom and says, This way.

So now she'll be crunching down the gravel path, between high banks of bramble on each side. Exclaiming softly each time she slips in an invisible patch of mud. Ray should be marching ahead, not saying a word, not warning her as he turns sharply and disappears round a corner, so she scuttles after him, between the birch trees. A low bridge over a ditch and they come out at the corner of an open field. On the other side of the field is the river.

I go into the bedroom and look through the starboard porthole. A wink of torchlight. Or a spark on my retina. I open the cupboard by my side of the bed, the one painted with green roses. That's my cupboard. The rest are his. On top of my rucksack there's a folded purple pile, which I shake out into a long cheesecloth dress. Circles of blue sequins across the bust. It reaches my ankles.

I pull the studs out of my ears. When I arrived I considered hiding them, or telling Ray they were only glass, but eventually I decided just to wear them and not say a thing. Everyone these days wears costume jewellery, why would anyone think these were different? For now I replace them with two gold-coloured hoops; little blue stones hanging off the bottom of each curve.

ALICE FALCONER

This is cheesy, Ray said when I showed him the outfit. Spiritualists don't look like this anymore, they're in velour shell suits jumping around on stage, on TV.

Only in the States, I said. They don't expect that here.

I hear women's voices – two, not one – scrambling down the slope to the towpath. They're laughing, which isn't a good sign, Ray must have cracked and said something friendly. My breastbone feels like it has contracted, forcing my breath short and shallow.

'This way,' he says, right outside.

I rush through the galley into the saloon, find the candle stuck in the empty Cognac bottle, and light it. Then I slide round the banquette, so when they come through the double doors, the taller woman ducking her head, I'm behind the table. Ray slides in next to me so they have to sit on the other side, can't get too close.

'Ladies,' he says, 'this is Morgana.' We'd agreed not to use my real name. 'She's proper magic. Sees ghosts, spirits, everything. She can tell if something's coming to get you.'

The younger one giggles.

'Morgana, this is Kath, and Charity. But I bet you knew that already, didn't you, baby – Morgana.' His right hand, resting on the table-top, takes hold of a water glass, lets go and picks up a metal spoon. Then puts it down again, seemingly without him noticing. A nervous tic.

'I can't tell names,' I say. 'Only hearts.' Best not to oversell.

They pull up chairs. It's almost dark in the boat, I can see only flickers of their faces, but I hear the smack of the younger one, Charity, chewing gum. She looks about eighteen. Propping her chin in her hands, she stares down at the peeling varnish on the table-top. Kath, maybe twenty years older, has a glossy brown bob, perfect-looking, nicer than her daughter's strawberry-blonde hair whose split ends sparkle in the candlelight.

Charity leans forward. 'You look young. How long've you been doing this?'

'I might look young,' I say. 'But I sleep twenty hours a day, I only get up in the evenings, to do this. Takes it out of me.'

'Do we tell you what we want?' Kath says. 'Or do you just know?' She's the one to start with, then. Believes me already.

'I only know what the spirits tell me. Many are flying around here tonight. One of them knows you.'

Kath sits up straight. 'Who is it?'

'You've been very ill, she tells me.' Kath touches the ends of her hair. 'She's coming through a bit weak, but she says – stress. Maybe.'

'Yeah,' she says. 'Yeah.'

I look away for a moment and when I look back there are nets draped over Kath and Charity, a grey criss-cross of lines.

'Now she's telling me about herself,' I say, keeping my voice steady. 'She's a woman who was part of your family not long ago.'

Kath's hopeful expression doesn't change.

'As recently as a few years ago.'

No reaction. The nets tighten over her face and flesh presses up between the strings, like winding thread round your finger. My throat closes in on itself. I swallow and feel sick.

'As recently as ten years ago,' I say loudly.

Still blank. Fucksake. Is every woman in her family a hundred years old?

'She may have had cancer, or some form of—'

'Marlene, it must be Marlene.'

'Marlene's not dead, Mum,' says Charity, picking at the varnish, so that what was transparent lifts from the wood and turns milky white.

'It could still be Marlene?' Kath says to me.

'This woman is older,' I say. 'Quite a few years older. Your memories of her may be quite weak. Think back to your childhood.'

'Great gramma?'

'Who?' Charity says.

'Yes,' I say. 'Gramma – great gramma – is telling me about you. She says – you have a lot of photographs at home that need to be sorted out.' It seems probable that this will be true for most people, though if I do Charity I might have to adjust for digital.

'Haven't looked at them for years,' she says.

'She's in some of those photographs,' I say. 'If you can find them all, she'll be there. What else? There is tension. Some tension with a friend or relative at the moment.'

Charity glances at Kath for a second.

'Someone very close to you. Gramma says you should forgive each other and move on. She says life's too short. And she tells me about you, Charity, you don't remember her, but though you put on a front you can be insecure sometimes, especially with people you don't know.'

She shrugs, picks at the table-top.

'That's funny,' Ray says. He says it very quietly, so only I can hear.

'What questions do you have for Gramma, Kath?' I say.

Ray shifts his bulk. His chair creaks. And I remember when we first met, telling him something like what I just told Charity. Something very similar indeed.

My heart starts to beat so fast the paste emerald on my breastbone shivers.

'Kath?' I say. 'What's your question?'

Ray's sitting next to me, so I can't see his face, only his hands resting on the table. Thick pale fingers with tufts of dark hair above the knuckles. I look up, try to concentrate on Kath, on the pink lipstick still colouring her top lip.

'When's Nax going to come home?' she says.

Nax? I don't even know if that's a dog or a person.

'Nax – she's telling me that Nax is a child—'

'You could say that.'

I see Ray's right hand grasp the Cognac bottle, bring it towards him. The candle flame bends and light shifts across the saloon.

'A grown child, yours or someone close to you—'

'Yeah.'

'And he's in another country,' I say. Seems like a fair guess.

'You could say that.'

Sweat prickles my armpits. I wipe my top lip.

'I mean he's not all with us,' I say. She's nodding. 'He is quite unwell.' Nodding. 'He's had problems for a long time.' She frowns. 'Longer than you know,' I say. 'He's not well in his mind.' She's nodding, round-eyed. 'But he brought it on himself—'

'Oh my God,' she says, banging the table with the flat of her hand.

'Gramma isn't shocked by that kind of thing anymore. She says—'

'When's he going to come home?' Ray interrupts. 'They asked when he's coming home.'

A GEOMETRY OF GHOSTS

The net tightens round Kath's face and it bulges like cheese in a string bag.

'He needs to get his head sorted –'

'What's wrong with his head?' Ray says.

'Gramma's not sure what they call it nowadays, but he's not thinking clearly, he's not like he used to be, he's changed a lot.' In one of the other boats someone has turned on a television, and faintly I hear the opening tune of a popular soap, threatening to puncture the solemnity. I speak faster. 'You need to help him sort his head out.'

'She doesn't know where he is,' Charity says, folding her arms.

'Gramma tells me you still love him, don't you?' I say to Kath.

'Course I do.'

'He can feel the love you have for him – keep having it – keep feeling it. He will call you, in – not too long. When he calls, don't be angry. Be kind. Tell him you love him. He needs to do the rest.'

She's crying. She rubs her knuckle into her eye, wiping melting mascara across her cheekbone, gets to her feet. She doesn't say thank you.

Alice Falconer grew up in London, studied philosophy at Cambridge, and works freelance as a legal consultant. She received the Onoto scholarship in 2013. Her novel is set in and around the east London marshes.

RORY GLEESON
Rockadoon Shore

Extract from a novel

S O COLD. CHRIST ON A TRICYCLE IT WAS FUCKING FREEZING. JJ swam on his back and then again on his front and watched DanDan over the way trying to claw up onto the pier, reaching for the three girls who were standing shivering in the night air. Cath, Lucy and Steph looked down at DanDan, shaking their heads as he tried to grab their toes and their ankles, scraping his chest on the corner of the pier.

JJ felt his heart in his chest and his body in the water, the coldness of it rising up and down over his nipples as he bounced on his tippy toes. They'd never been this close to each other before, the group of them, never been so openly aware of each other's presence, of their bodies. There was something vaguely cinematic about what they were doing, all of them like this in the moonlight. Surely this was what he had been missing, the sense of being part of something, of being present in some significant moment that would stay with him for years to come. He shouted over to them.

—Coming in?

Cath waved.

—We'll be in in a minute.

There was something with her and him, JJ and Cath. He was getting a weird creeping sense of it, of something growing without him pushing. Steph nudged Cath and shouted.

—Actually, we might not.

DanDan roared and splashed them.

—What?

—Yeah, we've changed our mind. Too cold.
—The fuck?
JJ copped on, but knew DanDan was still in the dark. He was too easy, DanDan.
—They're joking, fella. They are coming in, aren't they?
Lucy bumped her chest with a fist then extended her fingers to him in a peace sign.
—Right on, brother.
—See?
Steph and Lucy and Cath all moved to change at the same time. Steph peeled off her jumper and threw it down at her feet. Lucy wiggled off her bracelets while Cath bent down and slipped off her pumps. DanDan whooped.
—That's right, ladies. Off they go.
Christ, he would go and ruin it, wouldn't he. JJ did a stroke or two away from them, towards the chains that sectioned off the bathing area of the lake. Steph spoke to DanDan.
—We're not undressing for you, Papa Bear.
Lucy had her top off and she beat her chest with both hands then raised one arm high up over her head in a Black Power salute.
—Fuck the patriarchy!
Steph ignored Lucy and looked down at DanDan in the water.
—Turn around and fuck off over there like a good fella.
—Fine, fine. I was joking.
JJ pretended not to notice as DanDan splashed a few metres away, then lay floating on his back, watching the moon through the mist that blew in wisps over the surface of the lake. Probably going to sulk now.
JJ needed to get warm, so he rolled into a front crawl and started to swim towards the chain. He just focused on swimming. Hand over hand, right foot left. Swim your little heart out you beast. He began to find his rhythm. With his eyes closed and his head crushed with the cold he kept his face down and reached up every fourth stroke for a breath. Splash splash splash splash breath splash splash splash.
He felt he could swim a mile just like that. More than a mile. Spend the rest of his life swimming like he'd learned in the pool where his ma brought him when it was just them, just the two

of them, their one time a week where they were together. Her watching from the viewing gallery and him with chlorine in his nose and mouth, choking but going hard at it because she was there.

He felt he could swim like that again now, hard and fast, out from the chained enclosure of the bathing area and into the great lake beyond, swim past the submerged trees and the islands and the crannógs. He could swim up one of the rivers and go all the way upstream like a salmon. JJ the salmon of Kildare on his way home to die, and all the people passing would try and fish him out of the river. They'd float pills and Druids and CDs, iPods and ham sambos with hooks in them, but he'd know better and continue on. None of it would be any use to him, not when he'd decided to die. He'd swim up and up against the flow and force of the river along with all the other fishes. He'd surge up through rapids and he'd jump over waterfalls, past fishermen and murdered bodies and secrets buried under silt. He'd go so far upstream he'd come up in the cool crisp waters of the mountain, go to the very top, maybe, to the highest peaks and perhaps there locate a secret lake for himself where he could die, but no, JJ wouldn't stop there, he'd be evaporated up, he'd lose his body as it swirled into steam and cloud and he'd be taken up into the clouds and float over the length and breadth of Ireland. He'd be beyond himself, part of something greater, part of the earth, and he'd no longer worry about where he was going or what he was doing or if he was wasting his life. He'd go up into the clouds and blow out to Kildare, and he'd swoop down to the family farm where his brothers would be sitting in their usual chairs, doing up their cars and drinking from massive two-litre bottles of cider and picking on someone who wasn't him, because he'd be gone, he'd be a cloud, and his body would be a million, million little droplets of condensation and he'd come down and rust their cars, put water into the petrol tanks of their fucking cars that they'd spent much more time on than they ever had with him and then he'd go in and flood the basement where his dad used to send him when he'd act up. He'd flood the whole fucking place and they'd scream at each other and there'd be no one to clean or mop and then he'd be back up into the sky. He'd turn around and come back, brush up the little streets of Boyle, make everyone who walked the streets cold and give them shivers, and then he'd surround the old house they'd spent the last three nights in and freeze DanDan in his bed but leave off Steph and Lucy and Cath because they were good. Finally he'd go and rain himself back down into Lough Key, rain every last bit of him down into the lake where he could re-form his body and start his journey again the way upstream. Re-form the body that was freezing now and his balls contracting up inside him, keep doing his front stroke, hand over hand over hand. But JJ was past the railings and the chain, into the lake beyond, still swimming. And JJ thought, why go back? Why go back at all? Why not keep swimming till his feet went cold and numb and he wouldn't go up into the mountains and swim upstream, he'd simply lose the feeling in his arms and sink under the surface, go down to the very bottom of the lake and drown and they'd never find his body. Just sink down, and down, and it'd all go away, but then Cath screamed.

—JJ! JJ! Come back. Come back. NOW.

JJ broke his head full out of the water for the first time, his lungs burning. Treading water, he turned and looked back. He'd swum under the chains and was about twenty or thirty metres gone outside the rails. Cath was there on the pier down to her bra and knickers, and Steph's and Lucy's heads in the water bobbing up and down. He considered keeping going. Just turn, throw another arm into the water and keep going. Keep swimming. He needed some time to himself. But Cath shouted again.

—GET BACK HERE NOW.

Such a simple request. So direct and honest. Yes. Yes, he would. He turned, and realising how tired his arms were, he did a sloppy breaststroke back. Then he was scared. The chains far away. His arms aching and his breath laboured, coming in gulps. The chains swayed squeaking above the water. He inhaled in a mouthful of water and gagged. Vomit rose up into the back of his nose and he felt water and bile flooding his nostrils. Just one stroke more, one stroke more. Get back to the chains. His legs could barely keep him afloat, they kicked weak and feeble. His left arm doggy-paddled as he left his right one stretched out before him, his eyes closed against the rising water that went at his mouth, trying to force its way in, trying to kill him.

He was almost down to his last stroke when he felt the chain slimy in his hands. He pulled himself into the post supporting the chain and spat into the water. He was safe. He pressed his cheek close against the rotten wooden post and tried to get his breath. Calm yourself. Christ. His arms so weak he could barely lift them enough to grab the post. It felt like there was something dead in them.

As he gulped the burning air down, opening his lungs, he wondered if the others had seen him. That was a concern, what the others had seen, or what they thought they'd seen. But Lucy and Steph were in the water splashing each other, DanDan going Arrrgh like a pirate. They carried on noticing nothing. Grand. Grand.

He could see the outline of Cath on the pier. Beautiful she was. There was moonlight on her white skin. Painted her shining silver against the black water. Cath looked at him from the edge of the concrete shelf. It seemed like a moment between them. Something tense he couldn't explain.

Cath jumped in with a semi-graceful swan dive. Her body slapped as it hit and the black water swallowed her. Lucy and Steph screamed WAHEY and shouted for her to come on play polo.

But when she surfaced, Cath was swimming towards him. A deliberate strong stroke. Half-fish. JJ'd already forgotten what it was he was feeling when he'd gone out beyond. Just a relief now. To be back. He smelled water in his nostrils and inhaled a little and coughed. ACH. Too much. The fuck was he on.

Cath slurped to a halt beside him. He couldn't see the details of her face. Her hair was wet over her head and spread out, floating around her shoulders in the water. She held on to the chain where it joined the mossy green post at the top. He could see the outline of her nose and her eyes in the dark but not much else, and he tried to hide in the shadow her head was making. Water dripped softly from the end of her nose. She waited a moment then spoke quietly.

—What were you doing?
—Swimming.

—You went out.
—Just for a ramble.
Was he? Had he been? Christ his heart was going so fast. He didn't know. JJ had no fucking clue.
—Were you?
—Course.
—You scared me.
—Sorry, I didn't mean to.
—Arsehole.
Cath was hugging him. Wrapping herself around him in the water. Her hair against his nose. Even in the freezing water she felt warm to him. He allowed her to hug him, and just a little, his left hand felt the curve of her back and his ring finger pressed the edge of her bra strap. She released him slowly and they bobbed together in the icy water.

Rory Gleeson has a big Dublin head on him. He is currently redrafting his first novel, *Rockadoon Shore*, about a series of small betrayals in rural Ireland. He is also working on a short story collection, *Space Mountain*, about the dispossessed and creepy residents of Dublin City.

IMOGEN HERMES GOWAR

The Merchant Mr Hancock, of 14 Union Street, Deptford

November 1787

JONAH HANCOCK'S OFFICE WAS BUILT WEDGE-SHAPED AND COFFERED LIKE A SHIP'S CABIN, whitewashed walls and black skirting, beam pegged snugly to beam. The wind sang down Union Street, raindrops burst against the windowpane, and Mr Hancock leaned forward on his elbows, cradling his brow in his hands. Rasping his fingers over his scalp, he discovered a crest of coarse hair the barber had missed. He idled over it with mild curiosity but no irritation: in private, Mr Hancock was not much concerned with his appearance; in society, he still wore a wig. He was a portly gentleman of forty-five, dressed in worsted and fustian, an honest match for his threadbare scalp, the silverish fuzz of his jowls, the scuffed and stained skin of his fingertips. He was not a handsome man, nor ever had been (and as he perched on his stool his great belly and skinny legs gave him the look of a rat up a post), but his meaty face was amiable, and his small eyes with their pale lashes were clear and trusting. He was a man well-designed for his station in the world: a merchant son of a merchant's son, a son of Deptford, whose place was not to express surprise or delight at the rare things that passed through his hands, but only to assess their worth, scratch down their names and numbers, and send them on to the bright and exuberant city across the river. The ships he owned – the *Eagle*, the *Calliope*, the *Unicorn* – crossed and recrossed the globe, but Jonah Hancock

THE MERCHANT MR HANCOCK, OF 14 UNION STREET, DEPTFORD

himself, the stillest of men, fell asleep each night in the room where he drew his first breath.

The light in the office had a murky cast to it, full of storms. The rain came down in sheets. Mr Hancock's ledgers were spread out before him, creeping with insect words and figures, but his mind was not on his work; instead he had drawn from his waistcoat pocket a greasy page with one ragged edge, folded into neat quarters. He had begun to smooth it out when there came a scuffling from the staircase outside the office.

'Ah,' thought Mr Hancock, tucking the paper away hastily. 'That will be Henry,' but when he turned around from his desk it was only the cat.

She was almost upside-down on the stairs, with her tail in the air, her hind paws splayed wide, and her brindled body stretching down to the landing where her forepaws pinned a squirming mouse to the floorboards. Her little mouth was open, teeth flashing in triumph, but her position was precarious. To right herself, he calculated, she must let go of her quarry.

'Whisht!' said Mr Hancock, 'begone!' but she snapped the mouse up in her jaws and pranced across the landing and out of sight. He heard the thrum of her dancing paws and the dampish thud of the mouse's body hitting the floorboards as she flipped it into the air again and again. He had watched her play this game many times, and he had always found her enquiring, open-throated cry unpleasantly human. He turned back to his desk, shaking his head. He could have sworn it was Henry coming down the stairs. In his mind's eye the scene had already taken place: his tall thin son, with white stockings and brown curls, pausing on the landing to grin into the office whilst all about him the dust motes sparkled. Such visions did not come to Mr Hancock very often, but when they did they always disturbed him, for Henry Hancock had died at birth.

Mr Hancock was not a whimsical man but he had never been able to shake the notion that, the day his excellent wife had died in childbed, his life had diverged from its proper course. It seemed to him that the life he ought to have had was continuing very nearby, with only a very thin bit of air and chance separating him from it, and every now and then he caught a glimpse of it as if a curtain had momentarily fluttered aside. In the first year of his solitude, for example, he had once felt a warm human pressure against his knee during a card game, and looked down in fond expectation of a stout little child hauling itself to its feet beside his chair. Why was he so appalled to discover instead the left hand of Moll Rennie creeping towards his crotch? On another occasion, he had bought a brightly-painted toy drum that caught his eye at a fair, and had carried it nearly halfway home before he remembered that no small boy would be there to receive it. The years had passed and still, every now and then, Mr Hancock might hear a voice carried in from the street, or feel some tugging at his clothes, and his natural thought would be *Henry*, as if he had had a son all along.

He never saw his wife Mary in this way, although she had been a great blessing to him. 'A most excellent woman', as he had thought to describe her on her gravestone, or else 'most estimable', he had not been able to decide. 'Dearly beloved wife of...' – but his sister had objected.

'Too much!' she said. 'Such an outpouring! And they charge by the letter. Have some restraint.'

He did not expect her to understand his feelings for Mary. She had been nothing much out of the ordinary – a shipwright's daughter, with heavy white thighs and four teeth missing on the top left – but she was kind and wise, and she had chosen to join her life to his. 'What a thing!' he had marvelled, giddy with the miracle of it, 'what a thing, eh?' – the dizziness of possibility, the mere notion that this happiness might be bestowed upon him. She was thirty-three when she died, a placid woman who had seen much of this world and was amply prepared for the next, and although Mr Hancock backed down on the inscription, he chose for her a headstone carved with a great ship, sails ever-billowing. He did not doubt where she had gone, or the possibility that he might one day join her there, and for him this was enough. He only mourned their child, who had passed so swiftly from birth to death, exchanging one oblivion for another like a sleeper rolling over.

Beyond the pages of his ledger, beyond the tops of the houses, the masts of tall ships swayed. Other merchants of his fortune

THE MERCHANT MR HANCOCK, OF 14 UNION STREET, DEPTFORD

had moved away: they opened shops and set up home in Soho, Mayfair, &c, for although Deptford had been convenient for their grandfathers' businesses it was not convenient for theirs. Perhaps if Mary and the child had lived Mr Hancock would have done the same, but alone he had no instinct for change. He gained a great comfort from watching the daily progress of the naval ships, and knew no life beyond the rhythm of the dockyard, where ships left gleaming and laden, and returned – when they returned – battered and ragged. He understood what it was to load one's faith and fortune on board a ship and push it off into the unknown. The man who awaited a ship was distracted by day and wakeful by night, prone to fidgeting, with a bitter taste rising in the back of his throat. He was snappish with his family or else overly sentimental; he hunched over his desk scratching out the same calculations over and over again; he bit his nails.

From time to time, however, there was something more. A man might intuit that one particular voyage was not only to be a success but that it would be *special*. It would change everything. If he were sensible he would know that such optimism was dangerous, and yet still he would go about his business with a perceptible smugness, and in his private moments he might be gripped by a great childish glee of anticipation. Mr Hancock did not set much store by these fancies but he, nevertheless, so late in his life, felt again a stirring of hope: the opening up of possibility like the first revelation of sunlight in a sky densely piled with clouds. He had received no word from the *Calliope*, which with the right wind he expected to return from Canton in the summer, but he had come to believe that its cargo would be of a very particular importance to him.

Imogen Hermes Gowar is a recipient of the Malcolm Bradbury Memorial Scholarship. She studied Archaeology, Anthropology and Art History at UEA before working at the British Museum. This is an excerpt from her novel. Set in eighteenth-century London, it chronicles the love triangle between a merchant, a courtesan, and a mermaid.

KATE GWYNNE
The Imagination Game

Excerpt from a novel

Chapter One

KATHERINE LOOKED THROUGH THE PEEPHOLE AND SAW A MAN'S JAW, DUSTY WITH STUBBLE. He was good-looking, even up close. Behind him, terraces fitted with photovoltaic panels mirrored a cloudless blue sky. But the street was empty. She let the cover slip back into place and opened the door.

'Bird! I came as soon as I could,' he said, pulling her into a consoling hug. He released her from his hold and she stood hesitating in the doorway, taking him in. Today the usually friendly face was grim. He wore a black beanie that was pulled down to his eyebrows, his hands tucked into a hooded parka. It was eleven o'clock in the morning on a Sunday in late November. There was intense light without warmth, as though the sun had been replaced by a tepid fluorescent globe.

Rhys Mendes appraised her with his knowing grey eyes. 'You going to let me stand out here for eternity? In this bloody icebox.'

She had another look down the street, both ways. An old man shuffled out of his flat, manoeuvring around the tangled leash of his bobtailed Spandor, its enhanced, copper-penny coat glinting in the sun.

'Come on, you big scaredy-cat,' said Rhys. 'It's just me.'

'Sorry,' she said. 'Come in, out of the cold.'

As he followed her downstairs into the kitchen, she tried to go over what she'd prepared in her head. She knew why Rhys had come. Akal was dead. She couldn't think straight.

'Shall I put the kettle on?' she said, trying to think of normal things to say.

Rhys walked over to the window overlooking the clumpy grass, the mounds of dirt and the over-preened azaleas. Beyond that, the canal looked like a sink of dirty dishwater. The surface of the water darkened as a shadow moved across it. A Sky Runner drone looking like a giant leggy insect skirted along the canal, the designated route for North London commercial deliveries. Rhys took a seat on the sofa facing her. She'd make a pot, she decided. Let the leaves sit and infuse, let them take their time.

'Soy OK?'

He nodded, but they both knew the real thing was too expensive to bother with. And she still didn't trust anything that began its life in a culture dish. She brought the teapot over before sinking into the armchair opposite him.

'Well,' he said. His cheeks reddened. 'There's no point beating around the bush on this, right? We've known each other for what, like twenty years? We're not cousins or neighbours, but we're cool. I mean, we're just normal people with mortgages and kids and bills to pay.'

Katherine nodded. She agreed with his perspective but not the examples. Rhys was separated with a four-year-old girl. She didn't have kids or a mortgage, and as of last week, she wasn't sure she had a partner anymore. They were cool though, as he'd always said. They weren't the bad guys.

'I wanted to give you fair warning. As a pal. I think the directors are going to pull you in on this.'

It was no surprise, under the circumstances. It's what she had expected.

'Can you really believe that pathologist's report? I mean, excessive gaming?' He looked at her with a face that seemed to be all bewilderment, but she couldn't be sure what exactly he knew. Rhys was on the inside, he'd been at Nanoplay for years.

'I really don't know,' she said. She could have just said 'no.' She could have told him her concerns about the cog files, but she needed to know more first.

'Well, from the looks of it, there's a lot of ruffled feathers. Crisis meetings with the board of directors, though no official company announcements yet. It's what no one wants to say, but I'll just go ahead and say it. Finding a connection between Akal and Animo Tzar wouldn't be that hard.'

'There's no point jumping to conclusions. We need to wait until they give us more information.'

'Come on, Bird, let's not pretend we didn't know that the nanobot injections could be risky? This is all such fucking uncharted territory.'

'There's certainly no manual. But until there's evidence to suggest an actual link, that's just speculation.'

'Bird, just tell me honestly. Is there anything I should know about the cog files?'

Rhys met her gaze, and Katherine felt him searching her eyes for the answer. She thought about the player profiles that she'd fastidiously, painstakingly put together, working many hours beyond those she'd billed for. Akal was an artist, dancer and pro VR-gamer – she'd demonstrated the most complex combination of outputs, the most vivid imagination, of all the candidates for the game.

'Look, just as the file shows,' she said. 'Akal could not have been in more optimal condition for the game.' It was easier to distance herself through psych terms than to recall the girl that she'd grown quite fond of. It was better not to remember the person who set herself down in the chair across from Katherine, a confident smile spreading across her face, her training clothes clinging to an enviable physique. 'It was as though she'd spent her life conditioning her cognitive skills and physical stamina for the very purpose of playing it.'

'I could take some cues,' said Rhys, patting his belly. He'd lost a few pounds though. He looked better than Katherine could remember. 'But maybe all that perfection was just a front?'

'Maybe we're looking for a reason when there isn't one? Sometimes strange, unexplainable things just happen.'

'Right,' he frowned. 'And we live in a world that's fine with unsolved mysteries?'

She couldn't think of anything to say to that, so she sipped her tea silently, knowing that Rhys couldn't sit for one minute without something to say. He could talk to a brick wall.

His gaze drifted back to the garden. 'Well, nice place. When did you guys move in?'

'I'm housesitting for the winter. It's a friend's.'

'Felix around?'

'No. He's gone – I mean he's away,' she said, getting flustered. 'Bought a one way ticket to Berlin.'

'Told you he was bad news.'

'I recall you taking credit for us getting together.'

'Yeah, I introduced you one night when we went for beers, right? Talented guy, but artists, hey?'

She looked out at the garden, averting his gaze. 'I'm sorry, I don't think I can go into it right now.' Her eyes settled on a tiny slipper outside, abandoned next to the sliding door entrance. Katherine had gained a master's in New York. Fran, the friend that owned the flat, had gained a rich husband and two kids, and now they went to Provence every winter.

'Yeah of course, sorry.' He put down his teacup, and sighed. 'Well, I guess that's it then? We sit tight like bookends.' He lifted his cup as though to cheers her sarcastically for the awful position they were in. The waiting game. 'The thing is, Bird, Nanoplay will stop at nothing to get Animo Tzar out on time. Launch is three weeks away. You and I, we're the brains. Hunter, the board of directors, they don't know the first thing about how this works. I mean, if we're somehow, even indirectly, responsible for Akal's death, we're fucked. We could be indicted.'

She'd thought about all this. What it could mean for her career. She worried about the paper she was meant to be putting together for Goldsmiths, the whole reason they had agreed to fund the research around the game.

'Do you think I haven't thought of all this?' she said. 'I don't know what else we can do, though, at this stage.'

'Well,' he said. 'I've started going through the game log and player database. Figured I should see if anything comes up there?'

Now she understood why he'd really come. It wasn't just for peer support. Rhys wanted her to know that he'd been going through her cog files.

'But I thought you said they haven't made any company announcements yet?' It made her nervous to think what was in those files, captured and memorialised. Even though she'd kept copies, Nanoplay owned everything, they could do what they liked with them.

'Have a guess at how long it takes to go through that stuff? It's gigabites of data. A week at least. When they ask for something, they'll expect it in hours.'

'You're doing the right thing,' she said, because she knew that was the right thing to say.

'I think I'll go into the office now, get a start on it.' He stood up. 'Thanks for the tea.'

'Who needs a Sunday?' she said, trying to be reassuring.

She walked Rhys to the door.

'Do me a favour, will you, bird brain,' he said, putting on his jacket. 'Take a break from those artistic types for a while?'

She watched him as he made his way down Noel Street, heading towards Angel to take a share-shuttle to South London. Not far along, he stopped, then looked for something in his right pocket. She watched him intently. When she saw him take out his beanie, she had to laugh at herself for being so paranoid. He pulled it down on his head, and tucked his hands back in his pockets, walking like a guy that might be off to deliver some furniture.

Katherine went into her study to continue to mark undergrad psych papers, but she couldn't get Akal out of her mind. Her hand wandered to the gestural screen fitted to her desk, and to her Propositions profile page.

The hair in her picture was the same as she had it now, white blonde and cropped at her ears. She was still listed as a tier-two user. That was an accomplishment, she had to admit, being a few months off forty.

She'd registered as Dr Katherine Bird. Her real title, though some users took it as an invitation for a game of psychoanalysis. As if that idea was so interesting! Lab coats and fishnets were for amateur lovers, not mature women. She wanted to be excited, in the same way she felt while watching Akal in the game, experiencing it through her, the adrenaline rising, the default network of the brain activating as she met each opponent in combat, mind against mind. She set her intention and, with relentless focus, she defeated them all to become the tzar, the game ruler. Akal played to win, that's what Katherine admired.

'Katherine,' said Agatha, 'you have a new message.'

She wiggled a finger in her ear: there was no sound coming in from the right. It did no good. The pearl-sized implant needed replacing. The voice of her virtual assistant continued on the left, so she made do with one.

'Confidential and high priority. Requires code to authenticate.'

'Sender?' asked Katherine, but she already knew.

'Nanoplay.'

'Animo Tzar.'

'Authenticating. . .' said Agatha. 'OK, you're in. The message is thirty seconds long.'

'Good morning, it's Hunter Breach here. You've all seen the news: we have a very serious situation on our hands. The board of directors has asked me to hold an urgent meeting at HQ, three o'clock this afternoon. All senior team members working on Animo Tzar are required to attend. If you're out of the country or have extenuating circumstances, that's not an excuse; please contact me directly so that we can make arrangements.'

The connection cut out. Katherine sat quite still, her hands resting on the cool, smooth feel of her aluminium desk. On the gestural screen, she pushed through web junk until she located her carefully organised cog files. She then had to pass layers of security authentication until PLAYER 8: AKAL DEVINE came up. She ignored the psychometric tests, transcripts and FMRI scans. Katherine was looking for something specific. She was looking for a recording of her final session with Akal.

Kate Gwynne is from Sydney, Australia. She has lived in Mexico, New York and currently resides in London, where she is working on *The Imagination Game*, a futuristic thriller. Kate also has a career in digital marketing and is UK Editor of *Tottenville Review*, a book review website.

LIZ HAMBRICK

St John's Avenue

An excerpt from a novel

NOBODY ANSWERED WHEN SHE KNOCKED ON KEITH'S DOOR. Maybe she would come back tomorrow. Or this afternoon. Then again, maybe she wouldn't come back at all. She would forget about Keith and his garden and put the past back where it belonged, where she could control it. Those were her sensible options, sensible as her shoes. 'Sod it,' she said, and walked round the back.

Keith's side gate could have done with some work, but the rotting post leant in her favour. With a quick shove she realigned it, pulled up the latch and walked through.

She tapped on the back door – the same geranium red hers had been – and listened. No sound came, no shape appeared so she tapped again, sharply this time. She wrapped her palm around the door handle, noticing the liver spots on the back of her hand. A bird began to sing, a garden thrush on the roof of the coal shed. The lock stayed put. She tried again with more pressure. The bird kept singing. She felt its eye on her. In the shed there might be something to force it with but there'd be spiders too so she rummaged in her bag for a nail file, or scissors, anything, and felt the sharp outline of the shrapnel through the lining of the pocket. It might be too crude a tool but she liked the idea of it so she lodged it between the handle and the wood of the door. The fit was tight. She put her weight behind it, ignoring the pinch on her skin.

The way the door yielded, the way the lock cracked so fast, it might have been waiting for that piece of metal alone. And then she was in the kitchen, the bright stillness somehow expanding the space of it. These kitchens had always been so full of natural light. She stuck the pinched side of her hand in her mouth, the taste of the shrapnel sharp on her tongue, and stood for a moment, listening, breathing.

The room smelled of sick and the never quite dry wood of the draining board, and of tea leaves, years of boiled potatoes and whatever film covered the lino. A towel lay across the chair where Keith rested the day before and a tin of soup sat on the table, a smear of tomato and fat on the underside of its lid.

She found the vomit in the sink. 'Jesus Christ,' she muttered and swallowed hard, against the reek, against the contents of her own stomach. Under a bowl and saucepan bits of carrot and potato speckled the enamel. Holding her breath, she squeezed in some Fairy Liquid and ran the hot water so it filled the saucepan and then the bowl, sending a quiet fountain of diluted soup onto the lumps to make a foul new broth of its own. She let it run, adjusting the flow to match the outpour of the drain.

She saw her mother pouring water for potatoes in the old days next door, the peelings in a sink strainer. She heard the clatter of a colander on a weeknight after school, saw the steam rising like a genie and the soaking of their draining board, a very slight slime always in the wooden grooves and crevices.

Keith had the same shelves they did. Hastily painted, a layer of dust had settled in the brush marks, but they were quality. They would stay on the wall until someone pulled them down, and not before. These old council houses were built in the days when things mattered.

Hattie picked up a strainer. 'You've got a mind like a sieve,' her mother used to say. And sometimes that was true, but not now. Breaking and entering had made it airtight. She stroked a collection of figurines. A cocker spaniel, a Dalmatian, a collie, all coated with grime.

The water ran cold. Hattie turned off the tap. She opened the cupboard that contained the immersion heater and flipped it on. While the sink drained she stood still, listening to the house, hearing only the plumbing the way it used to sound next door.

'Hello?' she called.

Nothing but the pipes.

'It's me, Hattie, your old neighbour.'
Silence.
On the bitter cold days – it was never any other kind of cold – they used to lug the oil stoves out, one to the kitchen with a kettle on the top, and one to the bathroom to stop the pipes from freezing. When she was old enough she was sent Down The Road for a gallon of paraffin. She could smell the oil shop now, the greasy tang, the faint damp forest trapped in the oak of the floorboards.
The hallstand at the bottom of Keith's stairs was lumbered with coats, all of them his by the looks of things. On the drawer sat the same phone, it must have been, that Keith's dad had used to call her that morning, the morning that had shifted from the long ago to the now. Two-tone olive with a dial, it was a relic. She ran her hand over the smoothness of the receiver and shivered. 'I've got some bad news, I'm afraid.' She caught her reflection in the mirror, the image both her and not quite her. She was the same age now as her mother had been, on the morning Keith's dad found her.
Eleven steps. Every time. Eleven on Christmas morning, eleven at bedtime, eleven when she climbed them in twos to the landing at the top, peeping at the Ottleys' back door beyond the busy Lizzie on the windowsill. And eleven the time she flew down them, not fell, but flew, levitated, bouncing only once on the sixth step. She remembered that impossibility, still convinced that she had flown, just that one time, when she was small and light and capable of defying the Earth.
Halfway up she stopped and called out again. 'Hello?'
Nothing.
She saw her mother sighing, so small as she gripped the banister tight, and already stooped at Hattie's age so that her cardigan gaped at the bottom.
The landing was filled with sun. English sun. Keith had a spider plant growing on his windowsill. It was happy there, at home, heavy with trailing offspring. In her house she would have turned right to get to the bedrooms but in Keith's she had to turn left. It was a small difference, a small price to pay for being otherwise at home in the sun on the landing this day in June, with

the hydrangeas and roses outside, the clematis and the lupines. It was home, really, as close as it gets.

'Anybody home?'

She entered the front bedroom first. A single bed in the corner, a night stand beside it and opposite, a wardrobe. Otherwise, nothing but dust particles in the sun. She could see the colours in them. If she listened hard enough she could hear them, space particles like fairy bells.

She found Keith in the second bedroom, the mirror of the room next door where she was born. She had to stifle a cry. He lay on his back, his mouth open, one hand limp over the edge of the bed and his head centred on the pillow, which was clean and uncreased and cradled him like a cloud. There was no sun in this room, just flat white light. To stop herself shaking she wrapped her arms tight around her body. She stood over him, looking for movement behind his eyelids, finding none.

'Keith. It's Hattie. From yesterday. From next door.'

No response. She would have to touch him, to feel for his pulse. She would have to call for help, her own pulse dangerous in her neck. She would pick up the phone on the hallstand, the weight of the receiver heavy in her hand, put her index finger in the nine and push it around, see and hear it revolve back, clicking, and then push it around another time, and another. 'I've found my neighbour dead.' She would say that out loud. She would hear herself saying it in the empty hallway.

But when she touched him he felt warm and when she looked closely the covers rose and fell. He looked peaceful, not with death but the oblivion of a deep sleep. He was alive. Her blood rushed back all at once and she let out a sigh for the ages.

He looked so much like his father, the nose and mouth and cheekbones and brow. It could have been him lying there, the same age as thirty years ago. She picked up his hand – it felt cool, not fevered – and placed it inside the covers, expecting the movement to wake him; but nothing about his breathing or face changed.

Hattie looked over the things on the nightstand. A book of crossword puzzles, a pair of reading glasses, a tumbler of water with bubbles clinging to the sides. And a prescription box of pills, a blister pack on top of it with two compartments popped and empty.

She had got herself into a fuss over nothing. Keith had gone to bed not feeling well and taken a couple of tablets to sleep it off. That's all there was to it. There would be no need to call the emergency services because there was no emergency. She would call a doctor, that would be all, get the number from the box of medicine. But first she needed to collect herself, to take a few deep breaths and wait for the adrenaline to wear off.

She went back into the small room, the mirror room where Keith's dad had found her mother cold. Hattie had not been able to say goodbye. They had advised against seeing the body. But she had imagined the pathologist's cuts around her mother's skull, blue and yellow and purple ridges on the waxy grey of her skin. She had not been able to stop herself. Hattie sat on the bed. Her weight shifted things and the dust danced frantically. She ran her fingers over the bedspread, a candlewick. Then she lay her head down so she was half on, half off the bed in the position her mother had died. Hattie closed her eyes and listened, trying to hear the sound of the intruder her mother would have heard, if she had been alive when he entered, and nobody would ever know.

Liz Hambrick was born and raised in London. She currently lives in the suburbs of Washington, DC where she earned a bachelor's degree in Creative Writing and the Social Sciences from George Mason University in Fairfax, Virginia. The rest of this novel contains some humour and illicit happiness.

NICK KIPLEY

Untitled

This is an excerpt from a circadian novel set in Southern California

5:40:00 AM

WHY DO THEY CALL IT TAXIING ANYWAYS? The plane came to a halt and the captain turned off the 'fasten seatbelt' sign. The cabin went a-rattle with the tinny maraca of three hundred metal couplers being undone simultaneously; as per British Airways company policy, Léo Delibes's *The Flower Duet* from the opera *Lakmé* began playing softly in the background. She looked out the window of the seven-forty-seven and noted the low tan buildings with the flat roofs; the flagellar palm trees whipped the sky with green rounds of applause. Her mother gathered up her little things and smiled wearily. She gathered her little things without breaking her gaze on the outside world. The scene filled the little oval window, but irritatingly enough, didn't fill it to bursting. And she wanted the little window to burst. She wanted to be in it already. Won't they hurry up and move? Don't they want to get off this plane? The mountains were desert purple. It reminded her of Egypt. The sky was Hollywood blue. It reminded her of nothing else.

She put on her socks and found her shoes. Everything was in motion but nothing moved on the aircraft. They'd yet to open the door. Couldn't they at least do that? No, probably not actually. She thought maybe she was acting silly. Her shoes weren't even on yet. But oh, how she was eager to breathe air that didn't feel canned and charged with the static fibers of cheap one-use blankets! At least they were near the door. Maybe twenty people.

UNTITLED

Back in London one could see – in a rainslicked kind of way – the sky in the ground at all times. In LA it appeared that the ground reflected the sky as well, but in an inverse way to London's nearly constant wetness. If you look at the sun for a split second, and then look at the objects around you, they look paradoxically washed-out and hyper saturated. That's the best way she thought to describe it. Everything looked like the after-effect of having been perfectly lit, constantly, for years.

She stood and her knees got sharp for a second, emitted tiny clicks and then felt a little like warm rubber. She raised her arms up over her head and stretched as best she could in light of the overhead bins. She'd taken her bra off before last night's uncomfortable attempt at sleep. No point in putting it back on until the hotel. She yawned. Her breath smelled like how mouths smell when you haven't had any need to use it for eight and a half hours. Dinner. That was the last time she'd talked. Vegetarian pasta. White wine. Then she'd pulled the blanket up to her chin and watched a movie about dragons.

Miles away at this precise moment, I closed the venetian blinds and began preparing for bed having stayed up all night and not gotten anything done. I put *Mythologies* back on the shelf and could hear the pigeons through the wall. It was that time of year when the pigeons did nothing but make noise in the roof. When I was a kid I used to throw my shoes at the corner of the ceiling to get them to stop. It worked for only a few minutes of silence before they'd inevitably start up again and I'd realized that I'd have to get out of bed and go get the shoes (which would keep me awake) or just tough it out and stare at the ceiling fan while listening to the pigeons, pondering whether or not it was worth getting out of bed to fetch my shoes (which would also keep me awake).

She turned her phone back on while an elderly man in the seat in front of her stood, removed his glasses and wiped his eyes with a belabored groan. Up ahead, the bodies began to move. She took one last glance out the little window.

As I brushed my teeth, I decided that I might need a haircut soon, while making foamy faces in the mirror. After I finished trimming my beard I put away the electric razor and pulled down my lower eyelid, a gesture of which I've never really been sure what the medical purpose is. I was reassured nonetheless when everything appeared to be normal, if not a little bloodshot.

Welcome to Los Angeles! a sign said, greeting her as she walked up the jetway (finally!) with her mom.

I got under the covers but, after a minute, kicked the covers off. Fucking pigeons. It was gonna be a hot one today, too. I could feel the heat rising from the garage.

She, while standing in the customs line, feeling sweaty and stiff but wide awake and electrically excited, fished in her bag for her passport (a blue bag covered in a pattern of white reindeer). 'SVERIGE,' the passport said. Her mother said something to her that, since I don't speak Swedish, I cannot write down. (Also, I'm not entirely certain how to make all the Swedish letters on this keyboard either. I can do the letters 'ä' and 'å' but cannot pronounce them; so, yeah, from now on picture every conversation between she and her mother in the best Swedish-sounding language you can imagine. Anyways…)

I stared mutely at the ceiling of my childhood room in my parents' house and considered the daunting amount of work still left to do on the dissertation I was currently undertaking for the University of London's English Lit program. I then considered that I should have probably done a dual degree in avian biology and organic chemistry; that way I'd know enough about pigeons to poison them to death successfully in the most painful way possible.

In both places, the fan blades hung from the ceiling re-and-recycled the air-temperature air.

I shut my eyes.

Her mother said something to her in Swedish and smiled. She awaited her turn to approach the booth of the next available customs officer and bounced a little in her shoes, typing something on her phone.

5:59:12 AM

It was hot and I had too many ideas so I got out of bed and turned my laptop back on. Following the initial whirring robotic-

UNTITLED

sounding noise of the hard drive kicking into electromagnetic gear, the speakers played what I've always assumed to be the final chord of the album *Sgt. Pepper's Lonely Hearts Club Band*. Then, an apple that someone had already taken a bite out of.

    I decided to check my email again. Sometime well after midnight I'd disabled the alert on my Mail application fearing that I'd be sent some more junk from Cracked.com (or some equivalent) in fear that I'd spend all evening browsing an endless stream of garbage-quality, list-formatted articles all sounding something like, '5 Biggest Mexican Sinkholes Ever,' or, '10 Reasons You're Not The Man Your Grandpa Was.'

    I'm always being sent junk mail when I'm trying to get work done and, like a dog whose salivary glands have been conditioned to react involuntarily to the ringing of a bell, the ping of receiving a new email always sends me off down some procrastinatory, tangential binge that *feels* productive because it's reading, but in reality is clearly just my amassing useless information (to be fair though, some of these articles are pretty fun in the speculative-fiction sense with the best one by far being, 'Five Inventions Probably Thought Up By Someone With ADHD,' which at one point (point three, I believe?) posits that some hyperactive cave-child manically rubbing two sticks together simply because he-or-she was 'probably really bored during an Ice Age blizzard' serendipitously discovers a practical method to create fire and thus revolutionized the course of civilization, etc.).

    The junk I sorted through this morning was all from Amazon-dot-co-dot-UK and Amazon-dot-com respectively, given my two most recent addresses.

    The door handle moved and the cat walked in. He's a large cat, able to open doors using his immense weight and large, gripping cat paws. He stands on his hind legs and yanks the door handle down and then sort of leans his way in. One of his favorite hobbies is opening all the doors in the house and then walking room to room meowing at the top of his lungs.

'Mrow.'

'What do you want?'

'Mrow. Mrow.'

'No, I'm busy; apparently this digital coupon will allow me

to drive an Aston Martin for thirty minutes if I only take the plane to London, then the train to Lowestoft, and then pay forty pounds and and also learn how to drive stick. Ooh. And this one is good for a free wheatgrass shot with the purchase of any bag of wild bird feed... Actually, what the hell? Is this a pet shop that sells smoothies? In *Pomona*? Yeah. I am totally *clicking* on that.'

'Mrow.'

'Ugh. We've been through this, Cat. You're not old enough for watercolors. You'll make a mess. Plus, what happened to your oil pastels? You were just getting good at those. That's totally your thing isn't it? Pick up a medium and then go dropping it the minute your initial creative burst runs dry and you're confronted with the daunting technical aspect of the craft.'

'Mrow.'

'Thumbs? What's that got to do with it. Da Vinci didn't have an ear and he still painted.'

'Mrow.'

'Van Gogh! Da Vinci! You know what I meant!'

'Mrow.'

'Touché, Cat. Touché.'

The cat circled my chair, rubbing his face upon each of the legs, 'Mrow.'

'Well I don't care what *all* the other cats in the neighborhood have and don't have. If I say you're not old enough then you're simply out of luck, pal.'

'Mrow,' he said, turning and leaving the room (then, softly, from down the hall), 'Mrow.'

'I heard that!'

My mom knocked upon the open door, hovered for a second in my periphery, and then entered the room.

'You're up early.'

'To some. For the Chinese I think it's still midnight.'

'What?'

'I haven't gone to bed.'

'Oh. Working all night?'

'Sort of.'

'What's that mean?'

UNTITLED

'It means I've only sort of been working. It's very difficult to stay focused. Look? This digital coupon will allow me to get something called a "Free Guacamole Hat," with any Mas Gorditas Por Las Familias Deal at The Taco Sweatshop. With values like these, I can't sleep.'
    'Oh. Well get some rest. You can read those later. You're gonna get sick if you stay up like this. It's going around.'
    'Going around? It's a gonna be a hundred degrees this afternoon.' (beat) 'Just where is it going around?'

'Carol Snowbread got it. She's been sick for two weeks.'
    'And which grade does Carol Snowbread teach again?'
    'Same as me. Third. Why?'
    'You're both around nine year olds all day. Of course it's always going around for you. Nine year olds are always sick...'
    'This is a bad one though. It's been getting teachers too, and you know how adults usually can avoid it? It's like a flu that gives you a really bad sore throat. Before school let out we had I think six absences in one week.'
    'That's where, like, the common cold came from I bet... from a pack of nine year olds. When I was nine I was sick *the entire time*.'
    'Go. To. Bed,' she said, turning and leaving (and then in that sing-songy maternal voice which nearly-always foretells disaster), 'or you'll *catch* it. Oh hi mister kitty kitty.'
    (faintly) 'Mrow.'
    'Traitor,' I mumble of mister kitty kitty.

Nick Kipley was born and raised in Southern California. He's 25.

JACQUELINE LANDEY

The Hunter & The Gatherer

An extract

THEY HAD BEEN SIPPING APÉRITIFS ON A ROOFTOP CAFÉ SINCE A LITTLE PAST EIGHT, when the sun dropped behind the mountains surrounding Lake Lugano, and the large looping letters of a Campari sign flashed pink at their feet. As the darkening sky flaunted star after star, Vic regaled Zoe with tales of business duels, quoting lines from feisty emails he had sent, gripping her thigh with relish when recalling a line he thought particularly well-rendered. Zoe chose to find it all endearing. She laughed and gasped in appropriate places, and at intervals, surreptitiously raised her arms to air her nervous, clammy pits. It was winter in Cape Town and by comparison Switzerland's heat was disorientating. All day felt as though she were leaning against a pizza oven, but as the evening drew on, the alpine air lifted the squelch of the mid-August heat.

'Vic, please, promise me it's a loan.'

He grinned, squeezed her knee under the café table. Even when angry, his mouth slanted towards a smile, a crooked lure in the stubble of his salt-and-pepper jaw.

She was on the verge of urging him again when he turned to summon the waiter, who arrived with Swiss efficiency, to order a third round of Aperol Spritz.

'Graht-see-eh!'

'Prego,' replied the waiter, slipping away.

Vic beamed, as if for a second they had all engaged in an Italian conversation.

Looking at him – at ease in his sailing loafers, side-parting more silver beside his suntan – she wondered if over their three-week separation Vic had grown more handsome. He ran a hand through his hair. Although cut back as he got older, Zoe had an old photo of him, circa '78, as a tanned shirtless hippie with dark shoulder-length waves, wearing the smouldering look of a young man of ideals. With his good sharp nose and lanky frame, he reminded her of Jesus. She teased that he was a version of how the Messiah might have aged. If a fifty-year-old Jesus had renounced poverty, worn linen shirts, taken up yoga, and used face masks every other Sunday.

'So, considering it *is* a loan, we'll obviously draw up a contract?'

Appearing not to hear, Vic traced the waiter swooping between tables. 'Signor takes his job very seriously doesn't he? Hasn't cracked a smile once.'

'He's too busy to smile. There's one guy serving this whole place.'

'I don't know. He looks rather dour. Reminds me of a Puritan.'

'He's probably just feeling short-changed. Placed at the wrong point in history and all. It's a pretty wicked point for a Puritan.'

'Ah, yes,' he slid his hand up her thigh, 'I better give him a big tip. Can't be cheap getting back to the sixteenth century. What should we call the miserable fellow? Who's a famous Puritan? You'll know.'

'I don't know. I can't think of anyone.' She tried to refocus. 'Um, Vic.'

'Um, Zoe.'

'Can we—'

With frustrating speed the waiter returned with their drinks: two goblets of tangerine bubbles, ice tinkling in the glass between blood orange slices. He placed a plate of warm focaccia bread, crisp onion and thyme flecking the crust. 'Complimentary,' he said.

Complimentary? Zoe thought. At this café, nothing was complimentary; the giveaways were built into the price.

'Prego,' the waiter repeated.

Prego, prego, prego. One day in Lugano and she had heard the word so often she was growing uncertain as to what it meant. It was like love, or fair trade, or terrorist.

'Mille graht-see-eh!' Vic smiled at the waiter whose expression remained deadpan as he picked up bits of broken tissue paper, shredded beside Zoe's butter knife. Vic slipped a note into the waiter's shirt pocket. He looked up at Vic, and with a smile tucked beneath his frown, nodded once, before walking away.

'See, a test. Not such a Puritan after all.'

'He didn't take it, you gave it to him.'

'A real Puritan would have resisted.' He leant in, his out-of-office stubble grazing her jaw. 'Zoe, he's a phoney,' he whispered, biting her earlobe.

'You know for someone your age...' She turned and kissed him scantily.

Zoe liked the attention Vic paid to waiting staff. It only occasionally edged on patronising; mostly she appreciated the way he never failed to look them in the eye, ask questions, toss in a joke, treat them like they were more than an extension of the kitchen utensils. She had waitressed for nearly a decade – through high school, university and the previous two years of part-time teaching – and believed you could tell a lot about a person by their restaurant manner.

'OK.' She looked at him directly. 'Assuming all goes to plan, I should be able to pay you back within a year, maybe two. Perhaps we should go over the numbers again, what do you –'

'Zoe, do you really want to talk about that now? Look at where we are.'

As though conducting a calming concerto, he gestured around the café: the rooftop graced with lithe, tanned women, and men in finely-cut suits, cat-walking between the bustling bar and the wrought-iron railing that she and Vic sat beside. In twos or threes, patrons would come over to the quiet, and in harems of secrets and cigarettes, admire the blue-blood lake below.

She ran her hands over the skirt of her dress, trying to smooth out its creases. 'Yes, it's all very beautiful. I'm honestly so grateful to be here, thank you Vic. It's –'

'No, no, Zoe, thank *you*. It's all my pleasure to have you here.'

'Still, if we're going to do this, I'd really like to clarify a few things, you know, interest rates, procedures if repayments fall behind, little things like that.'

Hearing the pop of a prosecco bottle, Vic's brows shot up with a grin, his eyes drifted to the railing where two women lit each other's thin cigarettes.

'Seriously, Vic, can we please –'
'Zoe, what's the problem exactly?'
'Nothing, I just –'
'Love, we're on holiday.'
'I know, I'm sorry to bring it up but –'
'I don't see what the urgency is about. Really Zoe, you need to trust me. And you do, don't you?' He let go of her hand and leaned back in his chair.

The waiter came by with a wooden board of pizza, trailing a heady twirl of oregano and garlic ribbons. Vic closed his eyes, tilted his head skywards.

'It's not that. I know this is an amazing opportunity and I can't thank you enough but I, I don't know, don't want to owe anybody anything. Or at least, I want to know what I owe them. And not that I think that you would use it.' Then almost into her lap, she said, 'I suppose we're all just trying to protect ourselves.'

When his gaze returned to her face, she felt as if he were tracing her bone structure, considering her nose, weighing up her flaws, deciding if he could stand them. In the few months they had been together, she had quickly learned that he not only had a way with words but also with silence, an ability to shell out moment after moment with a hollow quiet, gathering a power so thorough that when he finally spoke, she was so grateful for the words, she cared less about what they were saying.

With some hesitation, she put her hand on his knee, hoping he would take it. 'Of course I trust you. I just want to avoid anything going wrong. So if we put all the information on the table, in a contract, then we'll both know what we're getting ourselves into.'

'Zoe, I'm giving you a gift for Christ's sake. And here you are tearing out the insides before you've even unwrapped the wrapping. You know I'm not trying to generalise but I really don't understand why women are always analysing a situation before even trying it out. Lauren was the same. Always taking things apart while we were still bloody in them. Honestly, it's like prising nails from a rowboat while you're still sailing down the stream – just to see how it's made.'

She hated being compared to his ex-wife, or being put in categories in general: 'women', 'white girls', 'the youth'. It was their first night in Lugano. Perhaps it would be best to keep the peace, to swallow her questions and try to buoy up the moment: down her drink, praise his children, suggest a blowjob in the bathroom.

Reclaiming her untaken hand from his lap, she looked out at the now near-black lake, promenade lamplights treading the water's edge. Despite the breeze she felt feverish. She lifted an icy glass, rolled it over a collarbone inevitably blotchy with nerves, scalded by the sun after a day at the lido. She felt an urge to say something childish. Announce that she wouldn't have sex with him until they had signed a contract, but she knew he couldn't be bargained with. She suspected there was nothing she could give which he couldn't get from somebody else.

She felt her chest jump, surprised by his hand on her shoulder, taking and twirling a tuft of her honey-blonde hair. 'My love, I'm sorry. But I promise you have nothing to worry about. We'll talk business tomorrow.' He cupped her neck and with the surprising weight of two thumbs massaged her collarbone in small rotations. 'Come on, let's get the bill, looks like you could use a good night's sleep. We'll get you a gelato on the way.'

As they ambled along the lake, Zoe licked the smooth salt-sweet of the hazelnut gelato. The promenade funnelled into an arc of greenery, so the light around their footsteps turned mottled through the bramble.

'Smells like spring under here.'

Vic hummed in agreement.

'Wonder what kind of blossoms these are.'

He pulled out his phone, no need to wonder with these new smart cells. He began to thumb the touch screen. Zoe thought the whole concept was a bit weird. Why would anyone want to carry their office with them? She didn't see the fad really taking off.

'OK, so it says: "Lake Lugano is a blah blah blah." Ah, here, trees. "Lugano or Ceresio derives from the Latin cerasus, meaning cherry, refers to the abundance of cherry trees which one time adorned the shores of the lake." There we go – cherry.'

'It says one time, that doesn't mean still.'

THE HUNTER & THE GATHERER

He sighed and shook his head. He slung his arm over her shoulder, his gold watch loose on his wrist where the grey hair was beginning to show.

She hoped they were cherry trees. She didn't think she had seen one before, although the idea of them occasionally came to mind, alongside Rachel's words. Rachel was a jazz student and Zoe's housemate in second year. One night, drinking wine, they'd sat cross-legged on floor cushions in her bedroom, reciting poetry – in a play of pretension they both seemed to love. As the evening grew late, Rachel read Pablo Neruda aloud, said softly, 'I want to do with you, what spring does to the cherry trees,' as she, to Zoe's surprise, leant forward and kissed her red wine-chapped lips. And she continued to kiss her, and Zoe must have been kissing back. Then to the sound of whatever Cuban music they were likely to have been playing, they took off each other's clothes and she remembers Rachel climbing on top of her, moving slowly down her body with her open mouth. Zoe had kicked over a glass when she came. Remnants of the stain confessed on the carpet for months.

She thought about sharing the story with Vic but decided against it. He called her his little lamb, looking over her small pale body stripped down in bed, he said, yes, approvingly, quite the little lamb. Having only a trace of innocence to offer, she thought it best to maintain the illusion.

Jacqueline Landey was born in Johannesburg in 1985. She studied Art History at the University of Cape Town and English Literature at the University of Witwatersrand (receiving honours degrees in both). She has worked in journalism, education, and the art world.

ELSPETH LATIMER

Dog

A crime novel

My name's Jock and I'm 63, from Edinburgh. This is Dog. She's a stray I found outside my tenement. I gave her a bed last night. Don't ask about my work.

Extract from chapter one

AFTER BREAKFAST I FASHIONED A LEASH FROM A LENGTH OF HAIRY TWINE. When we got to the park, Dog tugged hard, her body twisting like she'd caught a madness off the grass. We should have stuck to walking round the block, less chance of Dog strangling herself. Soon as I undid the knot, she scurried to the nearest tree, squatted for a pee, then roamed further, sniffing, leaving messages. I stubbed out my fag and whistled, hoping Dog hadn't forgotten her new pal.

'Good lass,' I called, seeing a black shape race towards me. She circled a few times, then leaned against my leg, heart hurtling.

Sausages weren't proper food for a dog so we went to the shops. No dogs allowed. I tied her to a bollard. Once we were home I showed her both tins and she opted for the posh stuff. Dog chased her bowl till it was licked clean, then I gave her a treat from the butcher's, a meaty bone. I'd seen plenty over the years but none as big.

'Reckon it's dinosaur?'

DOG

Her tail thwacked the lino while her teeth gnawed and crunched. After she was done, Dog explored the flat some more, poking in cupboards. She found a dusty set of golf clubs, which Da used to take to Bruntsfield Links before his emphysema got bad. I pulled out a mashie niblick and practised my swing.
 'D'you enjoy a wee game?'
 She grinned, mouth open like a hinge.

Me and Dog made the most of our long weekend but on Tuesday it was time to meet my boss. We fortified ourselves with black pudding and set off, brass knuckles tucked in a pocket. Chilly for June, my bald patch was glad of the tweed cap.
 At Tollcross we joined the queue by the bus stop. Dog watched the traffic, not minding the wait. She looked smart in the red collar, bought yesterday, along with a leash and a rubber ball. I was hoping Stevie'd have a job for me this week. My wallet was parched.
 When the 16A came, Dog hopped aboard. I dug out my pass and a pound coin but the driver said pets were free. We sat near the front, Dog on my knee. Her breath smelled beefy. She peered out the window, ears swivelling, fit to come unscrewed.
 The bus took a half hour to reach Fairview. The doors wheezed open and we got off at the Plaza, a fancy name for a load of zigzag paving, bins, benches, and bushes in concrete pots. Folks were aiming for the shopping centre, leaning into a wind that wasn't there.
 I spotted Stevie Shites next to a huddle of trees. His dark hair was slicked back and he had on a tan Harrington.
 'Best behaviour,' I muttered to Dog as we headed his way.
 Stevie was eyes down, rubbing his mobile with two thumbs. He glanced up. 'Fuck's sake, it's the Invisible Man.'
 I was bored of this joke but did my usual smile. Dog whined and slunk behind my legs.
 'Got a scabby dog now? Fucking magic. Where'd you get that idea, you crafty old git?'
 Dog was company, nothing crafty, but I didn't tell Stevie. He preferred talking to listening. We crossed Gleeks Road then cut along by the canal. The water was like oxtail soup but smelled of plumbing.

'So, Jock, still keeping out of trouble?'
'Aye, Mr Steve.'
'I've got a job for you, a big one.' He laughed. 'Fucking enormous.' Stevie ran through the details, his Adam's apple jiggling the tag on his zipper. 'Do it Friday.'
'Sorry, Mr Steve, but I'll be at the Western.'
'Shite's sake, you and your fucking gall bladder.'

Next morning me and Dog woke early and were in Fairview by eight o'clock. Damp but no rain, thankfully. I found the street and we waited under a tree, Dog's nose hoovering roots. I kept an eye on the block of flats opposite. Its walls were coated in lumpy-porridge cement.

At five past nine a man squeezed out the double doors. Big Kenny was fatter than the photo on Stevie's mobile. His first stop was Munchies near the Plaza, for a bag of bridies, followed by betting in Win-Rite. He was never off his phone, even when eating. Dinner was kebab and chips at noon. Me and Dog shared a sandwich in a doorway.

From one fifteen onwards Big Kenny was at The White Feather, a bunker of a pub with orange glass beneath the eaves, like they'd a bonfire inside. I watched the entrance from behind the hedge of a boarded-up church. Dog had a snooze. Every twenty minutes Kenny came out for a smoke, never on his own, envelopes slipped between pockets. Business of a sort, not all of it friendly. I saw him spit on somebody. Chin smeared in gob.

After that, Big Kenny ate a stack of macaroni pies, then he hung about a different bookie's and had a fish supper, before another visit to The White Feather. When it shut he stumbled north, taking a lit path across a stretch of empty ground, with a few lank trees and nettles. Ideal. Far off to the left was a ridge of houses. On our right was the railway. This route brought him out near his door.

Me and Dog went home, slept, had breakfast at seven, and got the bus back to Fairview. By the afternoon there was no doubting that Big Kenny was a man of habits. Same places, same leery faces.

DOG

The hospital wouldn't welcome a dog so on Friday I left her behind with food and water. Machines took fuzzy pictures of my guts. A nurse wanted to know what I ate, then a doctor asked if I'd suffered any bad attacks. Hours of prying.

Soon as I stepped off the street I could hear Dog's howls in the stairwell. Poor creature must have thought I'd abandoned her. When I opened the door she leapt at me, licking my hands, cheeks, neck. It took biscuits and a lot of patting to calm her.

Dog was owed some fun. We went to the Links next morning with Da's clubs. I swung the mashie and her ball flew for miles. She sped off, legs a blur, and scampered back, teeth champing the rubber. We played for ages.

The two of us had a nap, before cooking a big tea. Kidneys in onion gravy. I changed into my dark trousers, then reached a fresh pakamac off the shelf and gave it a shake. Dog trotted into the bedroom, both ears perked.

'Sorry, pal, you've got to stay here.'

I was halfway down the stair when Dog started yowling. She'd not forgotten yesterday and being left on her own. The noise was enough to crack walls. I glanced at the door of the fussy pair who'd moved in last month. They'd soon be on the phone to the Polis. I couldn't risk it.

An hour later I was peering through the hedge at The White Feather. Dog sat by my feet, nose quivering, tail tucked round her bum. The pub was busy, folks coming and going. After ten minutes I saw Big Kenny. He wasn't alone. Him and his pals smoked their fags and went in again. Shame I'd not got this over and done midweek when it was quieter, but Stevie Shites said Saturday.

My knees felt stiff. Big Kenny would be on the booze till closing time, so we sneaked off for chips. No hunger, I only wanted the warmth. Dog ate a battered sausage. Her leash was trailing in the dirt, and I looped the extra round my wrist.

At twenty to eleven we returned to our hiding place. I rocked on my heels. Dog licked and nibbled her white paws. The pub finally emptied, Big Kenny among the last. A bunch did some drunken yelling then went their separate ways.

Me and Dog crept from behind the hedge and followed Big Kenny, not too close. Judging by his legs, he'd been on the whisky.

ELSPETH LATIMER

He started on his usual path across the wasteland, nobody about, just a few yellow windows in the distance. The railway wouldn't be a problem, trains didn't stop here at night.

It was dark but every thirty yards there was a lamp post. Big Kenny stopped by one and rummaged in his jacket, bald head bright as a Belisha beacon. While he stood puffing a fag, I led Dog to some bushes. She crouched and laid a turd.

Big Kenny coughed, spat, then chucked his ciggie.

I pulled Dog from her doings and we joined him by the lamp post.

'Whazzzit called?' he asked.

'Dog.'

That raised a laugh from Kenny, till he choked.

I waved a fag. 'Got a light?'

He fumbled in his pocket. 'Heeryoogo.'

As he coaxed a flame with his thumb, me and Dog backed off, into the gloom. She gave a wee bark, mistaking this for a game. Big Kenny stumbled after us, jabbing his lighter in my face. Three more steps then I slid my knife out, ducked his arm, and sliced his thigh. Up by the groin.

'Ooooh,' belched Kenny, hopping away. 'Ooooh, ooooh, ooooh.'

Too much blubber. All I could see was a pink welt, flashing through the slit in his trousers. I'd missed the artery. His arms flailed. I darted low, thrust my blade. Cut a bleeder this time, gushing wet. With a yelp, Dog bolted. Her leash yanked me round. The knife soared from my hand. Fuck.

The bastard grabbed me, hissing. Dog snarled, barked, and ran between us. I wrestled Kenny. Dog shot through the gap again. Kenny teetered, clutched my arm. The sleeve ripped.

Down went Big Kenny. He smacked the tarmac, flesh shuddering. No more movement, not even a moan. The leash was wrapped round his ankles. Trussed like a turkey. He lay on his side, blood creeping across the path.

'Dog, you're a marvel.' I lifted Kenny's feet and unravelled the leash. 'Job done,' I said, my mouth in a Christmas grin.

I looked at Dog. She was trembling from nose to tail.

'You poor thing.' I knelt to stroke her but she slid through my fingers.

Dog sniffed Kenny, and yowled at the red puddle by his leg. She gave it a lick. Must have tasted electric. Her body shot into the air.

DOG

Next moment, Kenny twitched and rolled over. A jet sprayed from his thigh, catching Dog, spattering my pakamac. I braced, fists ready, and heard a rasping sigh. Big Kenny's last.

Dog stared at me. Eyes black, whiskers dripping blood.

'Here,' I said, reaching a hand. 'It's only old Jock.'

She cowered and backed away.

'Home, I'll take you home. Just need my blade.' I trod on her leash, to pin her while I scoured the tarmac.

What was that? Dog's head veered left, ears pricked.

Echoes in the dark. *'Bam . . . ya bampot.'*

Christ. I grabbed Dog's leash. Her body was stiff, pointing up the slope. Those clumps on the ridge weren't bushes, they were folks. *'Ya bampot.'* Coming our way.

Couldn't leave without my knife, my lucky blade. I raked the weeds. Crisp packet, can of Tennent's. Dog whimpered.

Then I saw them, two lads and a lass.

Three could be a problem. Where the fuck was my knife?

Elspeth Latimer grew up in Edinburgh. She studied Architecture at Cambridge University and was Rome Scholar at the Accademia Britannica. After running an architectural firm, Elspeth moved to Norfolk and now writes full time. *Dog* is the first in a series of darkly comic crime novels featuring Jock and Dog.

FERDIA LENNON

The Sky, Which is All Men's Together

An extract from a novel

Syracuse, 412BC

1

SO GELON SAYS TO ME 'LET'S GO DOWN AND FEED THE ATHENIANS. The weather is right perfect for feeding Athenians.'
Gelon speaks the truth. For the sun is blazing all white and tiny in the sky and you can feel a burn from the stones as you walk. Even the lizards are hiding under rocks, poking their heads out from under rocks and trees as if to say Apollo, are you fucking joking? I picture the Athenians crammed in, their eyes darting about for a bit of shade, and their tongues all dry and a-gasping.
'Gelon, you speak the truth.'
Gelon nods.
We set out with six goatskins: five of water and one of wine, a pot of olives and two blocks of that smelly cheese Gelon's sister makes. Ah, it is a beautiful island we do have, and sometimes I think that if future days be gentler than present ones, I might just leave Syracuse and build myself a little house by the sea. No more dark rooms, clay and red hands, but the sea and the sky, and when I come home with silver fish on my shoulder I find my wife, whoever she may be, waiting and a-laughing. That laugh I hear it now, and it sounds to me a soft and delicate thing.
'Why Gelon, I feel so good today!'
Gelon looks at me. He's handsome with eyes the colour of shallow sea when the sun shines through it. Not shit brown like mine.

THE SKY, WHICH IS ALL MEN'S TOGETHER

He opens his mouth to speak, but nothing comes. We walk on. Even though the Athenians are crushed, their ships fire wood, and their unburied dead food for our dogs, there are still hoplites on patrol. Just in case. Hermocrates gave a speech not yesterday about how you can never tell with these Athenians; a fresh batch could arrive any minute. Maybe he's right. Most of the Spartans have left. Word is they're heading for Athens itself, all set to siege it up right and proper. End this war. But there are still a few about. Homesick and useless. In fact there are four of them walking ahead of us now, their red cloaks trailing behind them like wounds.

'Morning!'

They look back. Only one of them salutes. Arrogant these Spartans but ah, I'm feeling good.

'Down with Athens!'

Two of them salute now, but there's no life behind it. They look tired and sad, like Gelon.

'I say Pericles is a prick!'

'Pericles is dead.'

'Aye, sure Gelon, I know that. I say Pericles is a dead prick!'

This time two of the Spartans laugh, and all four salute. Ah, I feel so happy today. I feel so, I can't explain it, but it's some feeling. Those are the best ones. The ones you can't explain, and we haven't even fed the Athenians.

*

Cleitus died last night. Paches and I covered him with stones, and I said a few words. It was a mistake. The stones, I mean. They kept out the rats, but now they're too hot and the body seems to be cooking. There are flies buzzing around the heap, but it's smoky too, a kind of brown vapour rising from the cracks. Before he went he made me promise I would see his family if I make it back to Athens. I said yes. We all say yes, and we all die. Last week Cleitus made the same promise to Callias, and before that Callias to Antikles. I've no parents, nor wife, nor children, so I wonder what I'll say. Look after my dog, Ajax. Make sure he's provided for. It seems a defeat to say such a thing, but it's true and I may have to say it.

We found a hole in the quarry walls. It was too small at first but limestone being soft we made it deeper. Two men can fit inside and the sun barely touches you. That's were I am now. Paches is beside me sleeping. We try to sleep during the day and look for water and insects at night. I don't know if it's best. You miss those Syracusans who come with food, but you also miss the ones who come with clubs, so perhaps it's best.

Paches's skin is red and flaking. There are blotches of pink scalp from where his hair has fallen out. You wouldn't believe that two months ago he was beautiful. Beautiful Paches. He says I'm the same. He says you can see the shape of my skull. That you can see the joins of the bone and that my eyes look huge. I lean over and rub a lock of hair that covers his cheek. It's still black, and a few strands come away in my fingers. He moans and opens his eyes. They're huge and green. All our eyes are huge. For a moment he looks afraid, but I whisper that it's me. I whisper that it's only me and that he's still beautiful. He's still my beautiful Paches, and he smiles and takes my hand.

*

'Which quarry shall it be today, Gelon?'

We stand at a fork in the road and a decision must be made. Gelon hesitates.

'Laurom?' says Gelon, at last.

'Laurom?'

'Yes, I think so.'

'Laurom!'

We go left. The path to the Laurom pit is a windy, treacherous thing. A coiling brown serpent is what Gelon calls it when the muse is upon him. We can smell the Athenians before we see them. The way being right twisted blocks a full view, but the smell is something awful: thick and rotten, the air almost misty with stench. I have to stop for a moment as my eyes are watering.

'Ah, it seems worse than usual.'

'That will be the heat.'

'Aye.'

I pinch my nose and we walk on. There are fewer than last time. At this rate they'll be all gone by winter. From a distance they look like so many red ants swarming on the rocks, though these Athenians hardly swarm. They just lie about or crouch, or crawl about looking for a bit of shade. Still to be fair, my eyesight isn't so good and some of those most stationary may in fact be dead.

'Morning!'

A few look up, but none return my greeting. Gelon ties some rope to a tree for the really steep bits and we shimmy down real easy.

Now there are some in the city who feel we've made a mistake. That keeping them here in the pits is too much, that it goes beyond war. They say we should just kill them, make them slaves or send them home, but ah, I like the pits. It reminds us that all things must change. I recall the Athenians as they were a year ago: their armour flashing like waves when the moon is upon them, their war cries that kept you up at night, and set the dogs a-howling, and those ships, hundreds of ships gliding around our island, magnificent sharks ready to feast on our island. The pits show us that nothing is permanent. That's what Hermocrates says. They show us that glory and power are but shadows on a wall. Ah, and I like the way they smell. It's awful, but it's wonderful awful. They smell like victory and more. For every Syracusan feels it when they get that smell. Even the slaves feel it. Rich or poor, free or not, you get a whiff of those pits, and your life seems somehow richer than it did before, your blankets warmer, your food saltier. You're on the right track, or at the very least a better track than those Athenians.

'Morning!'

A poor bastard sees my club and raises his arms. A stream of words follow, most of which I can't understand, his voice being a faint croak, but I pick out 'Zeus', 'please', and 'children'.

'Fear not,' says I. 'We come not to punish, though ye Athenian dogs do deserve punishment. Gelon and I are merciful. We come—'

'Shut up.'

'What Gelon? I speak the truth.'

'Just be quiet.'

I chuckle.

'Ah, you're in one of those moods, I see.'

He's already kneeling by the poor bastard, giving him water.

'Any Euripides?' says Gelon.

The man is sucking at the goatskin like it's Aphrodite's nipple, some of the water trickling down his beard. He's pink. Actually pink. Almost all of them are pink, though some are even red.

'Euripides man, do you know any?'

The man nods and sucks some more. Other Athenians are coming forward now. Their feet clanking with chains. There are more than I thought, though still fewer than last time.

'Water and cheese,' says Gelon, 'for anyone who knows lines of Euripides and can recite them! If it's from *Medea*, or *Trojan Women* you'll get olives too.'

'What about Sophocles?' asks a tiny creature with no teeth. '*Oedipus Rex*?'

'Fuck Sophocles! Did Gelon mention Sophocles? You—'

'Shut up.'

'Ah, Gelon. I'm only saying.'

Gelon starts with the terms.

'No Sophocles, nor Aeschylus, nor any other Athenian poet. You can recite them if it pleases you, but water and cheese are only for Euripides. Now, my man. What have you got?'

The man who was drinking clears his throat and goes to straighten up. It's a sorry sight. Try as he might he can't do it. His neck flops, the head swaying from side to side, loose fruit blown by a gentle wind. He begins:

'Eh, but we must learn to understand, King Priam knew...'

He stops.

'Is that all?'

'Sorry, I knew more, but I can't seem to. My head, it's broken see, I forget faces and I can't remember my... I swear I knew more.'

The man puts his head in his hands. Gelon pats him on the shoulder and gives him one last sip. I think the Athenian's crying, but he still sucks away at the goatskin. Water pouring into him even as it pours out.

'Can anyone do better than that? A mouthful of olives for some *Medea*?'

Many volunteer, but when it comes to it most fumble and pause, and complain about headaches and thirst, or just collapse on the ground so that we only get a line at a time. Two if we're lucky. One bluffer starts doing a scene where Medea is being

THE SKY, WHICH IS ALL MEN'S TOGETHER

wooed by Achilles, which even I know is a load of bollicks. Medea was way before Achilles. She was with Jason.

'But swift footed Achilles it can never be! O Hellas, my father will never allow it. Achilles what can...'

Gelon raises his club and the bluffer slinks away. Another takes his place. This one at least mentions Jason, but it's a bit Gelon already knows. Still he gets a few olives for his troubles.

The day goes on in this way. The sun gets fatter, yolkier and its heat less fierce. Pinks and reds bleed into the blue. I leave Gelon to it and take a stroll around the pits. Officially I'm scouting for actors. Gelon's taken a bold step and offered to return with two sacks of grain if he can get five Athenians to do act three of *Medea*. But he wants them to act it out properly. Perform it. He'll be lucky if he finds one. These poor bastards are just waiting to die. I imagine the worst spots of Hades are something similar. Hairy skeletons with a hint of skin. Apart from the hair, which is sparse, the only bit of variety to be found is in the eyes. Glassy gems made brighter by dying. Massive browns and blues peer out at me. I haven't found a leading man yet, but I'm looking.

Ferdia Lennon is from Dublin and studied History and Classics. He is redrafting a novel set in contemporary Dublin and Paris, a chapter of which was a prize winner in The Sean O'Foalain Short Story Competition, as well as working on a second novel set in Ancient Greece.

ISA LORENZO

Memories of a Forgotten War

An excerpt

Manila, August 1941

'**BE STRONG CELIA,' PAPA SAID, AS SHE WATCHED HIM PACK HIS THINGS.** 'Take care of your mother while I'm gone.' He folded each shirt methodically, laying them on top of well-creased pants. Papa was short and wiry. He was very handsome, with a wide brow and well-defined lips.

'Yes, Papa,' she said. Celia was only fourteen, and the thought of Mama leaning on her was frightening. But she would do her best. She wanted to say so many things to him, like 'How can you leave us?' and 'Don't go!' Instead, she clamped her teeth on her lip, biting until she winced at the sudden pain. She carefully smoothed the wrinkles from Papa's shirts. He didn't pack much – only what he could fit into a single case.

'You know why I'm going, anak?' Papa said. 'I have to do my part.' Celia nodded. He was whistling. He seemed excited, as if he was going off on an adventure. She felt a sudden rush of anger. Why was he so happy to be leaving? She wanted to punch him or, at the very least, kick and scream. But she did nothing.

She looked at the bedspread, at the white Abel blankets folded on the bed, at the baul at the foot of it, at anything but Papa. If she looked at him, she would start to cry, and she would break the promise that she had made just minutes ago. The walls of the room seemed to squeeze in on her. She found it hard to breathe.

Papa hugged each of them in turn – Celia, Luis, and Berting. He saved Mama for last. She clutched at him, and he whispered something in her ear. When she stepped back, she was smiling, although her lips were trembling.

Papa hoisted the case and looked at them. 'Well, I'm off then.' They followed him as he walked out of the house. They stood just outside the door, and watched him grow smaller and smaller as he walked down the street. Berting tried to run after him, but Mama held his hand firmly in hers. She wouldn't let him go, no matter how hard he tugged. Papa turned the corner and walked out of their sight.

Once he was gone, the house seemed smaller, quieter. Celia had never realized how reassuring the sight of Papa reading the newspaper in the morning was. He would drink his coffee and carefully turn the pages, nodding as he perused the day's news. She sat in his chair and looked down the table. Five empty chairs looked back at her.

'Taya!' Luis and Berting were running down the stairs. Luis was pretending that Berting could outrun him, even though his longer legs could easily catch up with his brother. At thirteen, Luis was way too old to be playing with Berting, who was eight years younger. But he had humored him ever since Papa had left. Celia suspected that Papa had told him to look after Berting, and for this she was very grateful.

An hour later, bodies heaving with sweat, the boys flopped onto their stomachs in the garden to play marbles. One side of the yard was now pockmarked with holes. Luis was good at this game. With a flick of his finger, he could send a marble straight into its designated hole. His favorite marble was made of white glass, which surrounded a cloud of green. He had won this marble from Patrick Santos, their next-door neighbor, after a long, pitched battle.

Mama never seemed to mind their antics. She didn't even scold them for trampling her beloved ferns while they were looking for beetles. In Papa's absence, she had turned to her garden. Every morning, she checked her ferns, carefully snipping the brown, withered leaves. She talked to them sometimes, although Celia could never understand what she said. Whatever it was, the ferns must have liked it, because they grew strong and healthy.

Mama tended orchids as well. Celia's favorite were the Cattleyas – their petals were a delicate white, with a smatter of yellow inside their frilled center. They were so soft that she hardly dared to touch them. Sometimes, she would stretch a finger out to stroke a petal lightly, while looking around to check that Mama wasn't there to see her. If Mama had an especially good one, she would take the flowerpot inside and carefully center it on their dining table. It made Celia happy every time she looked at it.

While Papa was away, they were left to fend for themselves as best they could.

January 1942

'The Japanese are coming!' Celia, Luis, and Berting ran outside. First, they heard the ominous thud of numerous hob-nailed boots marching in cadence. Then they saw them. The foot soldiers were dressed in full battle gear, with bayonets attached to their rifles and nets from which leafy twigs sprouted. Celia thought that they looked like funny little trees.

After them came mounted officers clad in white shirts and olive caps, jackets, and pants. The lines of soldiers seemed to go on and on. It was as if a tidal wave were slowly but inexorably engulfing the city.

'Those are the high-ranking ones,' a woman next to Celia whispered. As she scanned the long row of men, her eyes settled on a face that looked vaguely familiar. The soldier was middle-aged, yet the way he held himself, stiff and straight, belied his years.

Berting suddenly tugged at her hand.

'That's Mr Ona!' he said. Celia felt a jolt of recognition. Mr Ona looked strange without his apron. What was he doing with those soldiers?

'Spies, all of them.' The woman next to her hissed. Celia started. She hadn't realized that she'd spoken out loud. The woman kept on talking. 'The furniture vendor who sold me a narra table two years ago just rode by.'

Berting waved as Mr Ona passed by, but the soldier pretended not to see him. They had stopped by Mr Ona's ice cream shop every Sunday on their way home from church. Mr Ona, who sometimes gave them an extra scoop of ice cream for free, was now the enemy. How could this be?

Celia glanced at Luis. 'Look at those guns!' he said. Then he looked around and remembered himself. He tried for a careless shrug. 'They'll be beaten in six weeks.'

She opened her mouth to contradict him, then decided that it was better not to say anything. She felt a frisson of fear. This army had driven the Americans out of the country. It didn't look as if they were going to be beaten easily.

Most of them were short, and smelled funny, of sweat and something rancid. They wore brown uniforms with baggy pants. The first time that Celia walked past one, he stopped her and said 'Kura-kura!' in a strange, high-pitched voice. She looked at him, uncomprehending. He tapped the top of her head, indicating that she should bow to him. She did. He pushed her head down, until she was bowing from the waist.

One week after the soldiers arrived, Celia and Luis were on their way home. As they were about to turn the corner to their street, they heard a shrill 'Kura-kura!' followed by the sharp crack of palm against flesh. A man had walked blindly past a Japanese soldier. Most men took the slap, eyes cast down, but this one was defiant. He drew his fist back. The sun shone on the soldier's bayonet as he drove it rapidly through the man's body. It was as if he was simply spearing a pig. Celia stood still, watching the man crumple to the ground. The soldier gave the body a contemptuous kick. She knew that she should get away before he turned to them, but her body refused to move. Slap. Fist. Bayonet. Body. Her mind was whirling.

'What are you doing, Ate? Let's go!' Luis grabbed her hand and began to run. She ran along with him, still replaying the drawn-back fist in her head, followed by the sudden flash of the bayonet.

After they saw the man's murder, they kept to the eskinitas, where they travelled as often as possible in order to evade the soldiers walking around the main streets.

ISA LORENZO

Three weeks later, Luis came home empty-handed. 'The bakery's closed. Mang Tonio said that there's no more wheat. People were standing outside the bakery with empty bayongs. Some of them had been there for almost an hour, but they didn't want to go home in case, by some miracle, pandesal magically appeared. They looked like fools.'

Celia was dismayed. She loved to eat pandesal with American cheese or Australian Cow butter for breakfast, along with a cup of steaming tsokolate. She enjoyed spreading the rich butter onto the warm bread, feeling it melt into the soft dough with each stroke of her knife. When she had put enough butter on, she would bite into the warm crust, then sink her teeth into the bread's pillowy center, and relish the sweetness of butter and pandesal.

She had already set out the butter and cheese, but now she put them away. She took out the tsokolate canister, opened it, and peered inside. There was only a little bit of tsokolate left. She decided to have one final cup.

After she finished it, she sat forlorn at the empty table, trying to ignore the insistent rumble in her stomach. She sighed and went to the shelf of cookbooks. She picked one and opened it. Its pages were filled with recipes that had been rendered useless. They called for milk, eggs, beef, ingredients that had disappeared from the market.

This cookbook was now her favorite book. She read it whenever she felt hungry. She turned its pages slowly, running her hands over the colored illustrations. The cookbook's leaves were faded and wrinkled, but that didn't matter. She said the words to prepare lechon out loud, as if it were an incantation. Clean the pig. Rub it all over with salt and pepper, soy sauce, and condensed milk. Roast it. It conjured up memories of her last birthday party before the war. She had quickly bitten into the succulent, crackling skin, relishing the salty tang of flesh and fat. She had eaten so much lechon that it had made her sick. She hadn't eaten a bite of pork since the occupation began. She groaned. If only her stomach could be sated by words and pictures. She looked around the living room. The wood gleamed golden in the morning sun. But the table was bare. There were no longer any orchids to console her. Mama had replaced her flowers with a vegetable garden.

At first, Celia had protested when she saw Mama taking the ferns out of their pots.

'But Mama, they're so beautiful.'

'Beauty won't keep us fed,' Mama replied. There was nothing more that Celia could say. She helped Mama uproot the ferns and tear the orchids from their driftwood perches. She felt as if she were desecrating a shrine. Mama was silent as she ripped the ferns from their pots. Her hands worked briskly, efficient in their cruelty. Celia thought of the many hours that Mama had tended those plants, how carefully she had snipped off their dead leaves, and prodded the soil to see whether it was moist enough for them. She had even talked to her plants, as if they were her children. Celia swallowed. She willed herself not to cry.

Isa Lorenzo is writing a novel about the continuing traumatic effects of World War II on Manila and its inhabitants. Born in Manila and raised in California and Quezon City, Isa worked in journalism and development before turning to creative writing. She has been published in *Outpouring: Typhoon Yolanda Relief Anthology*. She was awarded the Malcolm Bradbury Memorial Bursary

JOHN PATRICK McHUGH
A Family Matter

IT WAS THE BLOOD ON THE JACKET THAT MAC REMEMBERED MOST. How dark it was and how much darker it made the black leather look. It dripped down from the studded collar, along the right sleeve and it hung from the golden zipper and teeth. It was like the jacket had been shot rather than his uncle. He would remember that bloodied jacket more clearly than the roar of his grandfather's shotgun, or the cries of his howling mother, and even more clearly than the ripping open of Patrick's face.

After the shot, when his uncle lay on the wooden floor of his grandparents' hallway, his arms stretched out like a faceless Jesus, Mac did not grieve. Hunched against the kitchen doorway, he could see his uncle was dead and gone. His brain and pieces of skull were on the walls either side of his body, sliding down just above the skirting board. But that jacket, that jacket seemed like it was alive. Wounded and bleeding, but still alive. Mac knew he could save it.

Mammy was screaming at this point. Screaming as she searched for the telephone. She was on her knees, her shaking hand having knocked the phone off the table in the hallway. Paddy's oozing blood stained the sleeves of her pink dressing gown as she frisked the floor. Not wearing her glasses, she was practically blind and when she was drunk, it was even worse. Mac's grandfather, Frank O, was walking back to the kitchen, after giving his son a good kick to make sure he had finished the job. Droplets of blood were splattered on his fat nose and forehead and his right eye was plum-coloured and closed. He winked at

A FAMILY MATTER

Mac as he passed. The sharp stench of whiskey hung off him and the double-barrelled shotgun was tucked under his left arm, bright specks of crimson staining its barrels. Mac watched as Frank O sat in the wicker chair beside the stove and placed the shotgun tenderly between his legs, before he found himself drawn back towards the dying jacket. He had to act fast.

Mac took two unsteady steps forward. He was pissed, blurry-eyed and an acute pain throbbed in his right temple; the hangover was already hitting. Deciding to give up on his legs, Mac slumped to the floor. There, after taking a deep breath which sent some of Patrick's blood up his nose, Mac began dragging himself towards the jacket. Blood was now spilling onto its torn cuffs, and the battered elbow pads were soaked in the red juice. Mac stopped when he heard voices coming from the kitchen.

Frank O was up, filling the kettle. He was singing an old rebel tune to himself and his right shoulder looked far larger than the left. They would learn later that his shoulder had dislodged during the recoil of the shot. Grandmother was kneeling and praying on the floor beside him. Mac could just see her slippers and skinny legs peeping out from the arch of the door. Her voice was loud as she spat out the words as Gaeilge: 'A Naomh-Mhuire, a Mháthair Dé, guigh orainn na peacaigh, anois, agus ar uair ár mbáis.' Black and white photos of Collins, Jack Charlton and the Virgin gazed down from all corners of the room and the window was wide open, letting in the mid-morning breeze. Mac's father Billy had awoken too, naked, upon hearing the gunshot. He stood in the kitchen doorway looking in at his brother-in-law, smiling at his corpse, nodding and smiling. Mac began again to drag himself towards the dying jacket.

That bit closer, he could really see the damage. The whole middle of Patrick's face was gone. It looked like mince, pink and purple mince. It was just a hole, and then Paddy's wild hair. When he was alive, Patrick would never pat down that hair, never wet it into place. It was always sticking out like weeds on a road. It suited a half-missing face, Mac thought, that hair. But the strangest thing about Patrick then, apart from the half-missing face and the gore and blood, was that he looked OK. His jeans were not full of the usual stains of grass and ash and they didn't smell much of piss. He had a new shirt on too, which was white (before the blood) and his fingernails, usually full of dirt or baccie, had recently been cleaned. And the leather jacket, though wounded, looked so noble. Mac almost thought the body handsome.

Wisps of smoke still rose from Patrick's face. He was dead the poor fool, poor Paddy, but the jacket was still alive. Mac gently pulled the sleeves free from both arms. There was still warmth in Patrick's skin and when Mac got past the stink of smoke and fresh blood, he could smell the alcohol. Once he had the sleeves free, Mac began to push his uncle over slightly to his side. An empty naggin rattled in the back pocket of Patrick's jeans as he started to move.

They had shared it only an hour ago, the two of them already pissed. Laughing outside the house, drinking it straight. Both happy and dancing in the dawn light. He was always good for a naggin was Paddy. Mac remembered getting one off him the morning of his First Holy Communion. Paddy and Mac drinking it with a can of 7 UP. Laughing away then, too. And Mac remembered Father Murphy knocking the host off his tongue once he smelt the stinging scent of booze. But sure that's the way it goes, Mac thought, Paddy is gone now. Like his uncle before him and his great-grandfather before that.

Mammy was still moving like a blind cow on the floor, but, as Mac got to work on saving the jacket, she had found the phone and held it to her ear. Wailing louder than before she called the Guards. Repeating, 'It was my own brother and father, *Mary and Joseph*, my own flesh, *Jesus, Mary and Joseph*'.

Frank O suddenly shouted, 'Does anyone else want a cup of tea?'

Mac's father said he did. Still grinning away to himself, still naked. 'Two sugars, Frank O, plenty of milk now, please'.

The smug grin was soon gone when he saw Mac's pale and sweaty hands grabbing at the jacket. 'Ya whore, what the fuck you think you're doing?' He rushed towards his son, slipping in the blood as he did so. And that lapse was all Mac needed. Panting, Mac snatched hold of both sleeves, stood, and pulled the leather jacket out from under his uncle's back and legs. More blood seeped from Paddy. Darker, like red wine.

A FAMILY MATTER

Billy, his face half-caked in blood, launched himself towards the jacket and grasped hold of its studded collar. The two struggled before Mac wrenched the jacket free and punched Billy's crooked nose, feeling it shatter. His father fell backwards over poor Paddy's corpse.

Frank O was now in the doorway, stirring a teaspoon in his mug, Grandmother behind him folding and unfolding a hand towel.

'The tea is ready, folks.' Frank O nodded at Mac. 'Jacket will look well on you, Mac, once you get her nice and clean. Long few years ahead of you so, Billy.'

Billy shouted, 'He isn't fuckin' keeping it. I can tell ya that much. I'm not letting it happen again and again. Not with my own flesh and blood.'

Mac ran towards the living-room and backdoor. The jacket balled under his arm, its blood falling as he went. Onto the rug, the Sunday newspapers, and onto a few photos of dead relatives.

Outside, Mac sprinted towards An Sliabh Mor Donn. The mountain that stood behind the little house. That stood high above the whole of the Island.

The ground was marshy as he raced for the summit. All brown reeds and yellow clumps of ferns. And the mountain had a sharp slope so Mac moved with his left hand out in front, grabbing for any hold in the muck. He could feel the jacket's pulse getting faster and faster and he could hear his father cursing his name. He didn't notice the weather. It could have been raining or it could have been sunny. He just ran. Up and up.

At the top, he squatted and laid the leather jacket flat down on the earth. Taking off his shirt and using the flesh of his hands, Mac dried the jacket. Dried the studs and gold zipper and the wrinkled sleeves and the pockets and the elbow pads. He cleaned each inch with spit and made the jacket shine again.

Mac could hear from below sirens and the crunch of wheels on gravel, and the calls of Mammy, and the bark of Grandmother as she tried to listen to the wireless, and the sipping of tea as Frank O explained to the two Guards that it was a family dispute, a family matter, and he could hear still the blood dribbling out of poor Paddy's head.

Frank O would be arrested and released within two weeks, on the grounds of compassion or misunderstanding, it was never clear. He would die before the year was out, a very happy man. Grandmother would become senile and unbearable upon her husband's death and so a pillow would be placed on her head as she slept three days after Frank O's funeral. Mac and his family would move into the empty little house soon after. Billy would take up the farming, the shotgun kept above his bed at night. Mammy would drink, pray and steal Communion from the church. And Mac would open the lid of poor Paddy's coffin on the day of his funeral and kiss that hollowed face one last time.

But this was to come, and that day Mac was high above all chains of the future.

High above all, atop that mountain. The Island seemed to stretch out in front of him. It seemed never to end. An entirety of brown and bog and dots of white with rising smoke. Mac put on the jacket. Its blood was dry and crisp on his hands. It fitted as if Patrick had been minding it for him. And wearing that leather jacket, Mac saw what his kingdom would be.

John Patrick McHugh was born in 1991 in the west of Ireland. He was awarded the Corsair Bursary at UEA, and is currently working on his first book set on a fictional island off the coast of Mayo. His fiction has been published in *The Stinging Fly*.

LILY MEYER

Bats

THE BAT ROOM IS ON A REVERSE TIME CYCLE. Bats are nocturnal and we work during the day – our day – so we switch their morning and night, keep the colony dark between nine a.m. and eight p.m., but when we go in the room we hit the override and blast their eyes with fluorescent hell. Bats blink like people. They swoop out of the air, unfurl their translucent ears and cling to the cage bars, chittering and shuffling, as we snap on gloves and take the animal we need.

When you come to Rhode Island, I'll bring you to my lab. You'll be surprised by how cramped and messy it is, kudzu vine cables in the electronics room, beer bottles clinking in the recycling from the nights we work late. The X-ray tunnel looks like it's made out of tinfoil, and the computer screens sprout aerials like spider legs. I'll take you to Animal Care, suit you up to protect you from the rabies our bats don't have, and turn on the lights in the bat room. I'll unlock the cage, and as soon as you step inside you'll hear the wing beats and the hissing humidifier, feel the wind on your face as the bats spin above you. You'll tilt your face to see their horned noses and beady eyes, and I'll stand behind you, watching your thin braids slide down your back.

Right now I'm working with Gentle Ben. I've sent you pictures of him. Black fur, bald snout, wide nose flared on top like a gingko leaf. He's a *Carollia perspicillata*, Seba's short-tailed bat. In the wild they roost in caves or hollow trees, eat fruit, not insects. Most of our *Carollia* are bad flyers, wobbly and lazy after years in lab cages, but Ben works hard. Dmitriy and I have been training him to fly the X-ray tunnel, dropping him down its rubber maw three times a day and shooing him to the far end with slices of cardboard taped to broom handles. He barely needs the encouragement now, which means he's ready to fly on camera.

We have to operate first. Monday morning we'll wax the fur from Ben's back, slice his skin open and sew metal balls to three points in each shoulder. If the anesthesia doesn't overwhelm his heart he'll get a full day resting in isolation, silver sulfadiazine on the incisions to protect him from wing rot, and a quarter milligram of meloxicam in his food for the pain. Flight trials start Wednesday. We'll put him in the tunnel, set up our video and watch the metal move with his bones.

Ben recognizes me when I open the *Carollia* cage. The others scatter, hang far out of reach with their talons wrapped tight around the ceiling mesh, but Ben stays put. He trusts me. He lets me scoop him from his roost with the butterfly net or, more often these days, with my latex-covered fingers. His heartbeat rattles his thin body. Someday I'd like to handle him without gloves, even though he scrabbles, shits, bites when he goes right side up. I want to feel his downy fur, the hot rush of blood in his wings.

We all talk to the bats. When we hold them we coo close to baby talk, trying to soothe them as they struggle, and when we fly them we grunt, curse, mutter that if they don't give us twenty good wing beats down the three-foot tunnel they'll end up lizard food at the bottom of Animal Care. And I talk to them when I need to think. Anna caught me a few days ago, hanging feeders of mango pulp and monkey chow, telling the circling bats how much I miss you. She linked her fingers through the bars. 'You need a real girlfriend, Mike. One on this coast.'

I shook my head.

'Well, at least get some roommates. Bats don't count.'

Anna was a dancer before she studied bat shoulders. Jazz, swing, and modern, she told me. She spent two years at SUNY-Purchase studying choreography and performance before she blew out her right knee. ACL and MCL tears on the same fall. The surgeons reconstructed the joint, but you can see the injury in her walk. She doesn't limp, but she sways. Misses beats. Dmitriy and I got to this lab studying small mammals, skeletal anatomy. Anna wanted to learn flight. Dance is about takeoff and landing, she says, and she's done with landing.

Yesterday night, after we scrubbed down the cages and replenished the food and fruit juice supplies, the three of us went to the Grad Center bar, same as always. We shared five-dollar pitchers of Narragansett and discussed the wing-shape data Dmitriy had just finished collating until Anna slammed her hand on the table. 'We've got to stop. We have to talk about something other than bats or we'll go insane.' She cocked her head at me. 'Michael's heading there already.'

Dmitriy shrugged. 'I like bats.'

'You can't only like bats.'

'Bats and beer.' Dmitriy reached for our half-empty pitcher and poured out refills.

'We're going out tonight.' Anna sucked down the foam on the top of her glass. 'We're going to act like normal people.'

'Out where?'

'To a club. We'll find one.'

Dmitriy groaned. 'Oh, hell, no. I don't do clubs.'

'Come on. Don't be lame.'

'I'm lame, Anna. I'm so fucking lame.'

She narrowed her eyes at me, pushed a strand of blond hair from her forehead. 'Fine. But Michael, you're going to dance with me. Right?'

Our research is on the mechanics of flight. Bats have more flexible wings than birds or insects, more joints to bend, and crepe-paper skin that stretches against the air no matter where the wings fold. We call this compliance. Our lab is looking underneath the compliant membranes, under the muscles, trying to isolate the locking mechanism in the shoulder that gives bats the power to lift off. At least, that might be how it works. So much of science is not knowing. Wrong guesses, failures. You would hate it.

We left Dmitriy on campus, cut down Benefit Street in the humid dark and landed at a Water Street club with a balcony overlooking the metallic river, a Top 40 R&B playlist, and a two-for-one Sauza Gold special. We did three rounds of shots surrounded by guys with blow-dried hair and the hip undergrads laughing at them before Anna tugged me away from the bar. 'I want a cigarette.'

'I don't have any.'

'Then I want to dance.'

On the dance floor the speakers vibrated and yowled and my hiking boots stuck to the parquet. Anna wriggled her thin shoulders and nodded her head to the beat. Her T-shirt rose away from her jeans, showing a band of pale skin as wide as my thumb. She flashed me a grin as I shifted my weight from left leg to right. Bodies rustled around us, circles tightening, couples snaking their hips together. Next to one dim wall I made out three poles, each with a collection of heeled girls around it, rubbing their backs down the metal and laughing.

Anna was laughing too. She opened her mouth to speak, but the music was too loud and she motioned me closer. As I bent to her lips the tequila burned behind my eyes. 'Dancers are the worst in clubs,' she said. Her breath was warm in my ear. 'We never know how to act.'

'I think you're doing fine.'

'I'm better at it now.' She sent a shiver from collarbone to knees, hips swinging with the song. My field of vision was shrinking around her. When I'm drunk it's always sight that goes first. You know that. You've seen me trip over roots in the sidewalk, bang my shins on the corners of your bed.

The DJ switched to a song I half-recognized. Anna touched her bad knee and grinned. '*Homecoming.*'

'What?'

She edged closer, the mass of backs behind her pressing into the space that she'd left. 'The song.' She lifted a hand to my shoulder. 'Kanye. *Homecoming.*' As I nodded she moved her other hand to my waist.

It was easier to dance that way, easier to keep the beat in my body, move with the music instead of the alcohol whirling deep inside my head. It was disorienting to be so close to somebody. Her mint-and-lavender smell cut through the club grime of sweat, liquor, stale smoke. I could feel the warmth of her skin, the soft brush of her hair on my cheek. She arched her neck, tipped her face up. I lowered my mouth to meet hers.

Flight takes more parts than you might think. Bats use tendon and bone for takeoff, muscle and skin to flap and maneuver. It's not just up-stroke down-stroke. Their wings curve and flatten like kites, the skeleton bending to reduce drag. A bat can turn completely around in less space than its body occupies in the air.

I left Anna on the dance floor. While we were in the club it had begun raining, a thin drizzle that caught on my arms. I checked my phone, but you hadn't texted or called. It was still early for you, just after dinner. Cars skidded down Water Street, bass lines leaking through their closed, tinted windows. I wrapped my arms across my chest and walked back to campus fast.

The streets were full of drunk undergrads, most moving from party to party with their elbows linked, Solo cups in hand, some groping each other behind buildings or pissing in the bushes. None of them noticed me as I headed up Thayer to Bio-Med. I swiped into the back of the building, got two Brooklyn Lagers from our lab fridge and took the stairs to the bat room. The lights were on. I flipped the override and before long the bats woke up, spread their wings and began to chirrup and squeak. I sat on the floor outside the cage, cracked a beer and listened to them taking off.

When I woke up this morning the room was light. The bats were folded like umbrellas, roosting in clumps when they should have been awake, flying. The back of my mouth tasted like Styrofoam, and my temples were about to cave in. My shirt smelled like Anna. I imagined her curled in bed alone, arms tight around her bundled blanket. You in bed, one leg kicked free of the covers, one hooked between mine.

I got up, left the bats still asleep. As I walked outside I saw that I'd missed two calls from you in the night. You always forget the time difference. Three hours. I hope you remember when I don't answer.

Lily Meyer is from Washington, DC and graduated from Brown University. She is finishing her first novel, *Providence*, about a Philip Roth-loving mobster in Providence, Rhode Island. Her next project, *Condors*, is about CIA support of South American dictatorships.

NG YI-SHENG

TOYOL

*The first chapter of a crime novel inspired by
Singaporean legends of the undead*

FOLKS DON'T LOOK AT ME MUCH. That's fine by me. In my line of work, it's a gift to be invisible: to hover over some poor blurcock's shoulder, eyes following his every blunder till you've enough evidence to hang him twice.

Still, every now and again you get a client like this one. Face like an angel, body like a porn star. Smile like a killer rosebud, breath that somehow smells of jasmine, all wrapped up in a girl-next-door Isetan sundress. And you're ready to curse the moon and shit at the sky, 'cos you know she'd sooner look death in the face than blink halfway in your direction.

But I'm one of the good guys. And being one of the good guys sometimes means keeping your trap shut, as my partner says. And God, I owe that man. Haron bin Aziz, your mouth is one of the world's primary natural resources for bullshit, but you're my own personal saviour.

He's handling the client now. Patting her hand, giving her tissue to mop her eyes. God, I hate him sometimes.

'It's OK, Miss Chan,' he's saying, in that deep, chocolatey voice of his. 'It's a natural part of the grieving process.' He's in that long-sleeve batik number he wears so well, with that amulet and that ladykiller moustache. Probably wetting her panties as we speak.

Suddenly, she goes all stiff.
'What's that?'
'What's what, Miss Chan?' Still all mellow and rich.
'That thing on the shelf. That baby doll...'

'Oh that? I use it for rituals.'
Rituals my ass, I think, and crack a grin.
'Its face changed.'
I can't help it. There's this lady in the shop, this perfect ten-out-of-ten covergirl, and she's actually looking at me. What are the odds? Haron's getting twitchy, though, trying to figure out how to get her eyes back to level one.
'Let's discuss your case.'
'Its eyes are moving.'
'You're playing with fire, Miss Chan. You know we're not your typical detective agency. We deal with forces beyond the scope of what the police even dare to say they believe in, let alone control.' He fishes a cigarette out of his shirt pocket, lights it in front of her with only his fingers. 'We'll finish the job. No problem. But you ask too many questions, sooner or later you'll get an answer you don't like.'
Turns out my partner doesn't know much about ladies after all. Fundamental rule: the harder you bluster, the more they want the truth. She's standing up now, arms akimbo, trying to look bigger than she is. She must've been impressed by the fire trick, everyone is, but she's doing a pretty swell job playing it cool.
'Mr Haron. I'm your client, and I hired you because I trust you. I'd like that level of trust to be mutual. In other words, don't treat me like an idiot.'
Haron blows a smoke ring and rolls his eyes at the ceiling. Finally, he calls out, 'Tony? We've got a customer. Miss Erica Chan.'
A moment's silence.
'Say hi, Tony.'
I put up a teeny-tiny paw.
'Pleased to meet you, Miss Chan.'
She's in shock, but waves back. Not a bad start. No screaming or fainting and banging her head on the floor and bleeding into the magic carpet.
'Is he a...'
'A toyol. A stillborn baby, reanimated.'
'I thought they were made up.'
'Miss Chan, he's right here. How would you like it if I challenged your existence in front of your nose?' He's clenching

his cigarette between his teeth now, ruining the filter, like he always does when he's trying not to laugh.

'But he's a—'

'Partner. He's a partner in this agency, and a bloody good detective too. Cigarette, Tony?'

I've drifted off the shelf now, and floated over to his side so she can get a good look at me, in all my forty cm, three kilogram glory. A cigarette doesn't sound half bad, though I've never been able to do the rings.

Haron lights one up for me and sticks it in my mouth. 'There's weird stuff everywhere in Singapore, Miss Chan,' he continues. 'Everywhere in the world. More strangeness than you – or any guy out there – can handle on your own. Trust us. Shut one eye. We'll do all the dirty work. All you have to do is pay the fee.'

Finally, it looks like she's got the message. She sits down, spreads her skirt across her perfect thighs, and looks up at me. Nervous-like, but smiling.

'Good to meet you, Mr Tony.' And now her eyes are on Haron. 'I like to know what I'm getting into. I won't have to sign my cheques in blood, will I?'

'Nothing so corny.'

'Fine.'

'But payments in cash. Two fifty an hour, plus expenses.'

She doesn't flinch at the price. Rich kid, I think. She's got a nice handbag on her, too. Shanghai Tang. Glamorous, but functional. A mark of taste.

We're finishing up the paperwork when her phone goes off. She excuses herself and flings open the shophouse door, ducking outside to carry on talking. The last beams of the day beat in on us, and I instinctively swoop out of the way – it's just six o'clock sun, no harm done – and hover in the safety of the shade, letting her finish.

The azan sounds from the Sultan Mosque. She tries shouting over the classical Arabic, then hangs up and marches back into the office.

'I've got to go. When can you start?'

'Anytime you like, Miss Chan.'

'How about tonight? Nine o'clock? My place?'

And Haron's rising out of his chair, all gallant and gentleman-like, jumping at the chance to lend a hand to his damsel in distress. But her eyes dart around the room till she sees me, hiding in the gap between the door and the filing cabinet.

'I'll need all the help I can get,' she says. 'Perhaps Mr Tony could come too?'

Sure, I'm a monster. But at times like this, when the world smiles down on me, I just want to cry whoopee and turn a somersault, right here in the air.

Fishing Village
A fable

They say the city never sleeps. Not true. Once a year, on the hottest day of the calendar, when the air shimmers off the mirrored skyscrapers like pale flames; when reservoirs sizzle and air conditioners spontaneously combust; when grass-cutters flood their protective masks with the salt of their foreheads and bankers pull at their funky ties and sticky pantyhose; then even the best of us can do nothing else but set down our heads and snore.

All over the island: cashiers at conveyor belts, surgeons in their operating theatres and sisters in their cloisters; gamblers at their baccarat tables, firefighters on their poles, CEOs in their boardrooms mid-Powerpoint; even the discipline mistresses in detention rooms and the sergeant majors in parade squares; even the maids hanging out laundry on bamboo poles and pilots cruising at thirty-six thousand feet. Even they stretch their faces, put up one arm then the other, fold it into a makeshift pillow and curl up in place. Even they know that enough is enough is enough.

And while they whistle in dreamland, the bob-bob-bob of the tides somehow jerks, the shoreline sinks, and the seas around the island drain to reveal fresh sand, new shells, bleached corals. Like a boudoir curtain drawn sideways, the waters expose new nakednesses: a world of ancient horseshoe crabs and turtles scuttling amidst ugly derricks and trawler nets.

And there, in their huts of shipwreck jetsam, are the Orang Laut.

They are the original fisher folk. They who lived in the littorals of the island, housed in houseboats, their generations extending back for centuries before the settler folk came.

They who were brown and sleek and healthy, fed on a fat-rich diet of slippery bright souls. They who swam with the squid and fucked with the dugongs. They who wrote nothing, claimed nothing, built nothing, knew nothing save for themselves, till white man, yellow man, India man came.

If the historian should wake now in the nest of her office, lined with stacks of books and microfilms, she might tell you the fate of their tribes, drawn from obscurity into the commerce of the global emporium. She would say how they made their homes in the swamps, chopping mangroves for heat while their wives sold fruit and beeswax to sailors in the bay. How they drifted away, dying of smallpox or else sharing their blood with the landlubbers, stowing their hearts into flats, jamming their dreams into punch card clocks.

She does not know the truth. How could she, when she naps, peaceful as a corpse?

Besides, they look different now. See how scales have grown at the edge of their lips, how fins adorn the fringe of their toes and whirlpool-eyes and navels. See how their nostrils flare in amazement at the sunlight, mistrusting it as an allotrope of water.

But with a blink, blink, they recall their duty. Clambering into their sampans, they gather their tools and wait.

Then the wind rushes in, and like long balloons, their boats are aloft, hopping across the air, into the city, coasting through the mighty towers and steelworks, mere metres above the ground. They chuckle as their barks narrowly miss collision with construction cranes, concrete malls, playground equipment, abstract statuary, scalps of citizens still snoozing below. They clench their knuckles as the wind blows them higher, higher, flipping them wave-like, stringless kites. The sun bakes their skins and they laugh, the quiet, gurgling laughs of those whose years outnumber any heap of salt grains.

And they bask in the open air for a moment, gazing with wistful bliss at the land below them, all spiked and grey. But the sun is high and can go no higher. They must set to work. Before the hour is out, the harvest must be complete.

So they throw out their nets: and what nets they are, knotted from the finest of silks, more nimble than any worm or spider might purge from her belly. And they cast out their hooks, and what hooks, smaller and sharper than the spark in the eyes of a cornered cat.

And these traps fall. They fall into the laps of those of us sleeping below, at their desks and their workstations. They fall into our mouths. But we do not wake. We do not catch hold of these hooks and ride them, heavenward, to say hello. We only toss our heads, smiling undisturbed, as magic covers us.

But something is caught. Their nets become heavy, their fishing lines taut. And we frown a little as they reel in their bounty from above, as if, in our unconscious slumberland, something has been irrevocably lost.

The boats of the Orang Laut drift back downward. The waves blanket them as they pass.

The sky cools a tick, and as if on command, the city wakes. We gaze downwards at our hands, guilty that we have allowed ourselves this lapse of judgement. We reproach ourselves, privately promise it will never happen again, that it was not in character; that no one noticed anyway, therefore it never happened at all. We shall forget it ourselves by the evening.

And if the eyes of a few of us are a little emptier, our smiles more false, our chests more hollow, what of it? Nothing has truly changed. And look: our work is not even halfway done.

Below, they laugh at us, rustling the depths. They count and celebrate their spoils. But we shall pay them no heed. Whatever has happened, we are convinced we are none the poorer.

We can afford to be magnanimous, anyhow. We are wealthy sons and daughters of industry.

If something was taken, we are sure it will not be missed.

Ng Yi-Sheng is a Singaporean writer and LGBTQ activist. He is the youngest winner of the Singapore Literature Prize, and his publications include a novelisation of the film *Eating Air* and the bestselling *SQ21: Singapore Queers in the 21st Century*. He is working on a story collection and a novel.

NICOLAS PADAMSEE

NYE

An excerpt

IT'S TRUE, I COULDN'T SHAKE OFF THE CONCERN THAT SMASHING HIS HALF-SISTER on his birthday in his house might tarnish our friendship. That's the kind of guy I am, have always been. There she was, nuzzling up against me, her simper nibbling at my heart, and I stood thinking. Anybody else would have reached for a jacket, cadged a condom and led her to felicity untold. Where did I go? Back to my bed. Where did she go? Back to her boyfriend and her baby. Oh well, I'm sorry, darling, but what can I say? You met a thinker.

Larry Nixon's the name. Let me introduce myself. Luscious brown locks coated with D:FI D3struct wax, which conceal the virility of my eyebrows, brush my flushed earlobes and outcurve at the back; amber eyes; pitted and fiercely pilose cheeks; three-day stubble (thank God for BaByliss); a lower lip like wrung rope; and, the reason for my brooding countenance, substantial overbite. The sum of these features: a shamelessly raffish visage, I'd say.

Let's move down. Nothing of note on the neck. But the shoulders, oh the shoulders. They're home to a panoply of spots: sessile mounds, tension-bloomers, cerise flares, you name it. No cream helps. No lack or abundance of light helps. Trust me, I've prostrated myself beneath the most pitiless sun. And did it work? Did it fuck. I have my theory. I think it's the showers: those thirty-five minute saturnalias soothe the mind, but they desiccate the skin. Seriously. I'm telling you. Forswear them. I will too. We'll do this together. Ah, who am I kidding?

On to physique then. I'm tall. That's ineluctable. Six-one, last I checked. And I'm skinny: artfully skinny. Buying me a

NYE

turtleneck? XS thanks. Buying me a blazer? XS thanks. You won't find me in sloppy fleeces: try fedoras, try Oxford shirts, try black jeans, try Chelsea boots – and jewellery: the necklace *du jour* is the eighteen centimetre gunmetal double-chain choker; no New Age beads, no tribal bunkum.

Right. That's the basics felled. I'll rig up the background. I'm twenty-five, I work in greeting cards, I live at home. There we are. Additional details: the father's a bibulous life coach, the mother's a depressive part-time piano teacher, and the brother's a disabled World of Warcraft addict. Not the fab four, but, hey, we're a family. We keep ourselves to ourselves. We manage fine.

Sure, you say, but what's so special about *you*, then, Larry? What's *your* story?

Well, I was nursing my coffee this morning, reflecting on my solicitude, on my decision not to bonk Brett's half-sister, and it hit me.

Larry, I thought, you're an inveterate overthinker, you really are. Still, why always repine? The life of a cognitive creature is arduous – of course it is – but, man, you can cash in on your cross. In amatory affairs, you've come a long way in the last month. I mean, the lead-up to New Year's Eve was a bona fide climacteric. Let your mind loose on that: pen your tale. You've been wanting to give The Great 21st-Century Novel a bash for years. Now you have your material, your odyssey. Everything's in place. You've read edaciously, and, well, Lord knows you have no difficulty in angling the *mot juste*.

I nodded then. I'm nodding now.

Two packs of Camels repose on the window ledge. The ashtray is spotless. The lighter fizzles and flames. And a bottle of red wine – organic Cabernet Sauvignon – abuts the table lamp.

Shall we?

1

To the crescendo tinkle of the seven a.m. alarm, I stirred, relinquished my polar bear, threw off the duvet and scrambled out of bed. In the bathroom, I brushed teeth, sluiced face in cool water, lathered cheeks and shaved. Downstairs, I necked a raspberry-and-peach smoothie, had a lustrous piss and then shuffled into the shower. Half an hour later, splashed with the banana fragrance of body wash, the vanilla of shampoo and the coconut of conditioner, I emptied a bowl of Fuel muesli, while, in the background, a grizzled news presenter bleated on: something about the high street, something about shops slipping into administration.

The journey from Shenfield to Liverpool Street lasted twenty-three minutes: not long, then, and it wouldn't have felt long if the carriage hadn't been ill-equipped, rammed and frowsty. There was no chance of a comfortable seat. The key was not to seek a seat. The key was to jostle for a metal handrail, something to lean against, a nook for luxuriating over the *TLS* or the *LRB*. To let other suckers rove the train for the few inches of spare fabric, invariably sited between snifflers or paunchy herberts.

The tube was no more agreeable. There, success was squeezing on, inclining your head, clutching your bag. After six minutes on the Central line, I alighted at Holborn. Half an hour to spare, ample time for a coffee, a cigarette.

Ah, December: the month of niveous hopes, crackers and Lucullan meals was my third at Felicitations.

9:28. I stubbed out my cigarette, hauled open the black iron door, winked at Lizzie, our svelte receptionist, and sauntered to the lift. In front of a full-length mirror, I elevated my fringe, let it fall and then brushed some hairs softly from right to left. Once the wind damage had been suitably patched up, I stepped in, rapped the rutilant two. The floor was occupied by three teams: UK sales, European sales and us, the Scribblers. Together with five other saps, I had the perennial task of formulating sunlit witticisms, mnemogenic puns, bawdy tag lines. (A personal pinnacle was HAVE A HA PEA BIRTHDAY: the card's cover featuring a dehiscent pod from which rapturous peas were flying forth.) With the last order date for Valentine's Day having passed, our workload was thinning, so considerable time could now be spent on the intranet.

'Hi, Larry!'
'Morning, Ginger.'
The Scribblers: four men, two women. Unlike the sales reps, we had our own islands. On mine I had a laptop, a couple of cracked pens, a highlighter, the *COED*, the *COT*, *The King's English* and *The Collected Poems of Philip Larkin*.

Ginger sat to my right. She'd joined in August. How to characterise my companion? Well, she was large, but in an awfully agreeable manner: buxom, comely. A thirty-six-year-old single mother, her cheeks would mantle with excitement as she prattled on about her daughter's lunchbox, her ballet lessons, her forthcoming theatre production. I would nod politely, re-reviewing her rack. Of late we'd become acquaintances, even friends. Her father was a novelist, and, though not an artist herself, she could recognise a selfless soul and enthused over my formidable concinnity. I'd brought in CDs for her to listen to, Dylan, Cohen, and lent her some books, Faulkner, David Foster Wallace, Nabokov, all of which, with my imprimatur, she'd sucked up. Yes, we had a first-rate working relationship.

The others? Dmitri, a forty-one-year-old film buff with a stentorian voice and a penchant for khaki slacks and slippery leather jackets. Ralph, a bespectacled physics graduate, whose shirt pocket was stocked with two pencils, an eraser, a sharpener and a compass. Sarah, a pink-haired R&B fan, who'd inveigled Safari into auto-updating her Facebook profile every four minutes. And Brett, whom I lunched with: a mesomorphic grammarian well known for his outré T-shirts, his taste for marzipan and his weekly trips to the zoo.

I slipped out of my coat, set down my coffee and turned on my laptop. What have we here? *Larry, I fucking love your sentences! Larry, you should send this to* Rolling Stone! *Larry, when are you going to write your first novel?* Before spooring homophones, I would trawl through my inbox, rereading the emails I'd saved, reminding myself of the exact wording of my colleagues' encomia. *Larry, I wouldn't ever have been able to think of that! Supernumerary? You're shit-hot today!* Thereafter the morning dragged: listless rumination punctuated only by fitful messages from Ginger and bass-heavy YouTube links from Sarah.

I kept an eagle eye on the time. 12:30: I slouched over to Brett.
'Hey, I'm *sans* comestibles. Shall we hit the Rainforest Cafe?'
'Sure.'
'It'll be chock-full past one. We should head down now.'
'Nah. We'll be fine. Chill.'
'Let's roll.'
'Fifteen minutes.'
'Coat. Satchel. Sorted. We can have a smoke on the way.'
'Ten minutes, man. I want to listen to *Suicide Policeman*.'
'What?'
'It's Yuck's new track. Six out of ten in *NME*.'
'Screw that. Come on.'

Thanks to the promise of a family-size Rasta Pasta, Brett straggled behind me.

'Just going to pop to the loo,' he said. 'I'll be back in a sec.'

The venerable pre-lunch piss: I knew his bladder wouldn't betray me.

'Right.'

I hotfooted it to the kitchen, transferred Mother's mixed-leaf sandwich from satchel to bin, wheeled round, smoothed out the collar of my All Saints shirt and then marched into reception. Twenty to. At least ten minutes before every cad in the building would be here.

'Hey, Lizzie!'
'Hello.'
'How are you?'
'Mm. Yourself?'
'Oh, *comme ci, comme ça*.'
'Mm.'
'Had a busy morning?'
'Not really. A few calls.'
'Great. Manage to snatch some reading then?'
'A few pages.'
'Terrific. And what are you revelling in?'
'A book by. Erm. Oh, Khaled Hosseini. *The Kite Runner*.'
'Fabulous. Enjoying it?'
'Mm.'
'Marvellous.'
'Are you rea—'

'Me? I've just been rereading *The Seven Types of Ambiguity*. William Empson. What a close reader! He's one of the forerunners of New Criticism, along with his lecturer I A Richards, of course. Funnily enough, Paul de Man avers that Empson's also a forerunner of deconstruction. But. Anyway. Empson's dissection of the "Come, seeling Night" passage in *Macbeth* – oh, it's imperishable. The man writes with such elan. You know, I think you'd lap it up. I really do. If you want to tuck in when I'm finished, just let me know. This copy's a bit foxed, but—'

'Thanks.'

'Anytime.'

Larry, you beast.

'So. Did you have a pleasurable weekend?' I continued.

'It was fine. I went to a restaurant with my parents on Saturday and saw a film on Sunday.'

'Excellent. Which film?'

'*Friends with Benefits* I think it was called.'

Oh, Larry, you are in.

'And how was it?'

'Fine.'

Running out of material here though.

'Brilliant.'

Running out of adjectives too. Christ, Brett, how much coffee did you consume?

'Yeah. I like films. I ordered a Bergman box set last night: his religious faith trilogy. My favourite? That will eternally be *Through a Glass Darkly*, though—'

'Sorry, Larry, there was a line.'

Phew.

'No worries.'

I slapped him on the back: if you want to impress a woman, there's no substitute for tactile camaraderie.

'Well, it was lovely talking to you, Lizzie. Let me know when you want to borrow the book. I'll see you later on.'

'Bye, Larry.'

'See you.'

Settling into a colloquy on the use of 'should' in conditional and purposive clauses, we made our way to Shaftesbury Avenue.

Nicolas Padamsee is 24. He graduated from University College London with first class honours in Law, and he is a contributor to the literary fiction section of *Review31*. The novel he is working on is entitled *NYE*. It is a comic meditation on love, sexlessness and artifice in 21st-century Britain.

DANI REDD

Vore

An extract

This is an extract from the second chapter of Vore, *a novel. It is a dystopian satire set in London and rural Wales in the near future. Following several crises in the farming industry, most people now eat lab-grown meat, which is cheaper and more widely available. In-vitro meat growing technology is also being used in more sinister ways. The extract follows James, the farmer, on his illicit meat delivery round.*

JAMES PARKED THE TRUCK AT THE TOP OF THE STREET near a row of boarded-up shops, and walked with the chicken back down to Anne's. He'd put it in a carrier bag, and was glad there was no one around to be nosy about what he was holding. As he stopped outside her house, he was assaulted by a feeling of déjà vu. He felt sure that this was the exact same house she'd grown up in. That house had definitely had a red door like this one. But he couldn't be sure. These streets all looked pretty much the same to him, always had, satellite dishes sprouting like mushrooms from each small terraced house. Most times the younger ones moved away as soon as they could, but the older people stayed on. Probably there were some of them who had nowhere else to go, but he knew Anne stayed here because she was lazy. A few years ago she'd divorced her husband Davie, and with all the alimony she'd screwed out of him she hadn't worked a day since. She'd told him once that finding out about that eighteen-year-old secretary from Swansea was the best thing that had happened to her in years.

James's stomach was tying itself in knots as he rang the doorbell. He'd last seen Anne about six months ago, at someone's birthday do down the Oak. Had ended up next to her, squashed into the corner as her thigh pressed up against his, whilst she, pissed up as usual, had kept on trying to bite his ear. Everyone had been laughing and it had been one of those moments where he'd had to try and laugh along too, else he would have looked like a prick, and the joke would have been on him. Standing outside the door now he could hear the muffled sound of music, and several female voices shouting to each other over it. She was entertaining. Great. She was even more of a handful when she had an audience.

He took a deep breath and rang the doorbell again, keeping his finger pressed down on the buzzer until he heard the music stop and footsteps moving rapidly towards the door. Anne flung it open, and James stiffened as she wrapped her arms round him in a hug that pressed her tits up against his chest. When she pulled away he rubbed his face and noticed traces of a beige residue on his fingers. She had put so much foundation on that the top layer had dried out, and she was shedding it like someone afflicted with psoriasis.

'Gladys has been giving me a makeover,' she told him, fluttering her lashes at him so he could see the uneven blue smears on each eyelid. 'What do you think?'

'Yeah. Great,' he replied, thinking that if Gladys was going for the drunken clown look she was spot on.

'It's a bit much, but as long as she's havin' fun, like. Anyway, come in, come in.'

They walked down the small front hallway and into the lounge, where Anne ushered him onto a black pleather sofa. There was a sinewy woman with short bleached hair sitting on the chair opposite, who leant forward when he came in.

'Now who's this, then?'

Anne sat down next to James and wrapped a sturdy arm around his shoulder.

'This is my friend James, Gladys,' she said, loading the word 'friend' with significance. 'Nice looking boyo, isn't he?'

Gladys lent forward.

'Bit of a scruffbag. But he's got some lovely blue eyes on him.'

'He's ripped under that horrible shirt,' Anne said, running her hand over his stomach and then withdrawing it before James had a chance to push it away himself.

The two women cackled. James, trying to avoid Anne's eye, looked at the coffee table and saw on it a bottle of white wine that was almost empty, and two glasses, one with a scarlet imprint of lips on one side.

'Well, all right then love,' Gladys said as she staggered to her feet and drained her wine. 'I'll leave you two alone. You should give him a bit of that nice salami I bought over for you. Way to a man's heart is through his stomach.'

'And the way to a woman's moady is through her stomach too,' Anne replied, causing the two women to go off into fits of uncontrollable laughter.

'Not hers, though,' she continued to James a minute or two later, once Gladys had left the room. 'That woman bloody lives on nutroshakes. Hasn't eaten solids in weeks. Great for me though, because her man works in a deli in Cardiff, and he's always bringin' treats back for her, which she just gives to me. Glass of wine, love?'

'I can't. I have to get back. So here's your chicken.'

She took it off him, and he tried not to flinch as their fingertips touched.

'I'll put it in the fridge. Gladys brought me a treat over that you must try. It's a taster, all the way from London. The deli doesn't stock it yet.'

'I'm not hungry,' James said, even as his stomach rumbled and betrayed him. There hadn't been much time for lunch.

Anne raised an eyebrow.

'I'm gettin' you a snack. Wait here. I'll be back now. And there's no need to look so scared, James. I don't bite... unless you want me to, of course.'

Picking up the chicken, she left the room before he could protest. If she had paid him already he would have got out of there in an instant, but as she hadn't he'd have to wait. It was daft of him to get so wound up anyway – Anne was harmless really, he'd known her for years. Still, James moved as far into the corner of the sofa as he could, pulling a cushion onto his lap. It was beige, with a cross-eyed Scottie dog embroidered onto it and a mustard yellow border that clashed with the turquoise walls. A bloody ugly cushion, even worse than those fluffy zebra print ones on the other sofa. Perhaps it had sentimental value.

'What you doin' with Mr Peep's cushion?' she asked, coming back into the room with a baguette, a cured sausage, and a knife.

'Mr Peeps?'

'My Mam's dog. She keeps a cushion over here for when she comes round with him, so's he doesn't leak on the sofa.'

James put the cushion down hurriedly, and Anne snorted.

'You're a bit of a prude for a farm boy.'

When James didn't reply she sat down next to him, emptied the last of the wine into her glass, and began hacking at the baguette. After cutting some uneven slices of bread she moved onto the salami, slicing off the tip before making a second incision. A thin slice of meat curled away from the steel edge of the blade. Anne cut several more before taking a sliver of it off the plate, throwing her head back and lowering it into her mouth. Sighing happily, she began to chew noisily. James watched and tried not to shudder. He hated watching people eat, especially someone who chewed with their mouth open, like she was.

'Now you,' she said when she'd finished.

James knew she'd keep on at him until he did. He put a slice of salami onto the baguette and took a bite.

'Nice?' she asked.

'Can't taste much. Just bread.'

'Eat it by itself.'

The taste was pleasant enough – slightly too dry, but salty and well-seasoned.

'Is this neomeat?' he asked her. 'I thought you weren't into that.'

'Yes,' she said. 'But this is different. This is special.'

She was looking at him with an odd expression on her face, almost smugly, as if by eating the salami he'd unwittingly agreed to something. It put him on edge.

'What?' he asked, swallowing the mouthful and taking another slice.

'Do you like Silvio Gomez?' Anne asked.

Silvio Gomez was a Spanish actor. Even James had heard of him.

'Um, yeah? Why?'

'Do you remember that scene from *The Culling Fields*?'

'Which scene?' James asked, although he knew the one she was talking about. The one on all the adverts, of the actor topless on the beach, his body tanning slowly in the sun as sweat ran down the grooves of his enviable six-pack.

'Oh forget it, it's a girl thing,' she said.

'Why are we talking about Silvio Gomez anyway?'

'Because you're eatin' him, love.'

James stared at her, confused.

'What the hell are you talking about?'

'Neomeat isn't just made from clonin' animal cells now,' she replied. 'They can use cells from humans too. This is the latest thing – celebrity salami.'

James gagged and spat the mouthful onto the plate. The two of them looked at the small deposit of masticated human cells, rising from the pale china surface like a small red island.

'Anne,' he said faintly, looking at the salami. 'Exactly what part of his body is this made from?'

'Oh, don't worry, you eejit. They use muscle cells. From his legs and stomach, it said on the packet. And paprika, and green peppercorns.'

'Jesus. It's not that. It's just, it's just... cannibalism.'

'No it isn't,' she replied. 'It's not really his body though, is it? It's just pretend.'

'But why would I want to pretend to eat Silvio Gomez? Or any celebrity for that matter?'

'Wouldn't you want to "eat" out Candira Flattista?'

'Maybe. But not ground up into a little sausage, like.'

She laughed at him.

'It's not going to kill you. Have another slice and a glass of wine.'

James felt himself beginning to get angry. What the fuck was wrong with people? Had they started eating each other because they were bored, or were they just sick in the head? There had been something on the radio about that yesterday – a vore fetishist accused of murdering a prostitute so that he could eat her. The suspect had been taken in for questioning but they hadn't been saying anything new about it this morning. James had always thought that vore was just an internet fantasy thing, but he was being proven wrong. Anne wasn't the murdering type, but perhaps eating the celebrity salami was a vore-type fetish to her. All the more reason to get away as soon as possible.

'No thanks,' he told her, as he got to his feet. 'Let's settle up and I'll be off.'

Anne got up too. She reached into her jeans pocket and handed him some notes.

'There's your money.'

'Ta.'

'James?'

She took a step forward, so they were inches away. The orange line of her foundation stood out against the pale freckly skin of her neck. James tried not to flinch as she slid her arm round him, placing her hand on the small of his back, so he could feel the heat of her palm through his shirt. Gently, he removed it.

'Sorry, Anne. I can't.'

'Why's that then?' she asked.

'I'm seeing someone.'

He wasn't really lying. He'd met a nice woman recently; Tezzie, she was called.

'You're a dark horse. Anyone I know?'

'No, I don't think so.'

'Try me.'

'She's not from round here.'

'Well, she's a lucky lady. Bet you give her great meat deals.'

'She's a vegetarian,' James replied.

Anne cracked up.

'Good luck with that one,' she managed to gasp through her paroxysms of laughter.

Dani Redd was born in rural Somerset in 1987. She is the winner of the 2014 *Words and Women* short fiction prize, and is working on her first novel, *Vore*. She is the recipient of a studentship for UEA's Creative and Critical Writing PhD.

EMMA RHIND-TUTT

Separation

An extract

ONLY TWICE IN OUR YEARS TOGETHER DID I HEAR MY MOTHER MENTION LOVE. The second time was June 1975. I was twelve, gazing down at my grandmother in her open casket, which took pride of place in the living room of my grandparents' bright and airy Savannah home. My grandfather stood with one hand on the casket's rim and cried. Shaking her head, my mother said: 'Love is the only thing that makes life worthwhile.'

I doubt that my grandmother Martha ever made any such claim. Her death-stiffened face looked disapproving, incapable of affection, bearing out my mother's verdict of her as cold and resistant to love. She did not resemble my mother Luciana, my younger sister Etta, or me, her only surviving blood relatives. I remember her mouth particularly. It was sharply turned down at the corners, a parody of surliness. There were murmurs at the wake that the mortician had 'done his damnedest', but that it had been impossible to shift the expression of stubborn disagreement that my grandmother wore after – during? – her fatal car accident. It was the visage she presented to death itself, and to twelve-year-old me it seemed both appropriate and brave. 'She was the finest person that ever lived,' my grandfather kept insisting, as if he was contradicting somebody. Luciana and my grandfather stood next to the casket, hand in hand, for quite some time: his gaze lowered in devotion to the corpse; hers fixed almost warily on the assembled mourners.

Even before my stay at my grandparents' for Martha's funeral – my first and last visit – their house was familiar to me, at least from the outside. There was a photograph of it at home in England.

SEPARATION

The colours were washed out – by that time the photo was already about ten years old. Etta and I would prop our elbows on the deep sill of our living-room picture window, and ponder this alien milky-hazed world that somehow belonged to us.

208 Columbus Drive was set back from the road behind a palm tree and a white picket fence. The windows had dark shutters, and there was an elegant porch wrapped around the clapboard façade. Compared to our characterless 1960s brick box in Surrey, the Savannah house was beautiful, a model of domestic promise.

Just off-centre of the photo, in front of the porch steps, stands my grandfather, arms folded and chin raised. His right foot is turned out slightly, at an unnatural angle, as if he is about to demonstrate a dance step. He lost his right leg to shrapnel at 1000 feet over the Dutch-German border in 1943. This was universally known in the family, but as a simple fact rather than the often revisited memories of Martha's life. If ever I asked Luciana about it, she just said: 'The plane made it, thank God, or I wouldn't even be here.' It was she who took the photograph.

I have a distinct memory of arriving at my grandparents' house for the funeral: Luciana and grandfather amble up the front path arm in arm. My grandfather is rheumy-eyed with new grief, but sleek and silver-haired, more distinguished-looking in the flesh than in Luciana's photo. His uneven walk fascinates me, and I long for a glimpse of his artificial leg. Etta and I follow in silence, as if we are already part of a cortège.

'Here they are,' cries a large-bosomed woman as we enter the white-tiled hall. She surges towards us from the sunny living room. 'Luciana, look at you!' She gives her the sort of crinkly smile that hides not only what you are thinking but also whether you are truly smiling. 'So fine in that pink outfit.' I can't quite tell from her tone whether this is a good thing. 'So like your dear departed mama.'

'Now, now, Aunt Beth, my looks are all *your* side of the family,' says Luciana, her voice more southern drawl than I've ever heard it.

She introduces us to our Great Aunt Beth as Calliope and Henrietta. *Cally*, we insist, *Etta*.

'My, what your grandma wouldn't have given to set eyes on you all,' says Aunt Beth.

'Nobody but herself was stopping her,' snaps Luciana, and Aunt Beth gives a little gasp.

This is the first, but certainly not the last, reference anyone makes to the fact that in the thirteen years since my parents married and moved to England, my father's home, Luciana has not once seen her parents. Nor has my father, Edward, who has stayed behind in England. I miss him; I do not quite trust my mother in his absence.

'His patients cannot *possibly* spare him,' I hear her explain to people at the wake and echoing in my mind is his refrain of exasperation with her: 'You would test the patience of a saint.' Until I was about eight, I assumed he meant the *patients* of a saint. By the age of twelve, I can smile at my childish word-confusion though I am also beginning to understand that, like my father's patience/patients, Etta and I too are being tested, our upbringing an exam that we could so easily fail.

Martha's funeral service is held at Savannah's grand St John the Baptist Cathedral. Gazing round at the luminous white and gold interior, Etta nudges me and whispers: 'Incense is the smell of heaven rotting.'

I bow my head, a little bored and aching at the knees. My mother's ankles taper into sharp-heeled red shoes. She has changed out of her pink suit into a black dress that shows off her long girlish waist. The priest stands at the pulpit, grips the lectern as if he's about to embrace it. 'Martha's start in life was tough, and yet with God's help she rose above adversity and trials to be a fine wife to our brother Thomas, and raise a fine daughter, Luciana,' he waves a hand in her direction. Her eyes are downcast, but open, looking at her lap, where she forces back a cuticle with her thumbnail. 'Visitors from England', the priest calls us. I feel exotic, important. I ape the prayers, wanting, despite my exotic status, to belong.

After the service, we dash down the front steps through a heavy shower to the line of black cars that hug the kerb. We drive to the cemetery out of town, over flat marshy ground that merges with the mud-coloured sky until a blade of sunlight splits the clouds. We huddle round Martha's grave pit as if it were a glowing hearth.

That evening Great Aunt Beth invites us to sing to cheer up our grandfather. I scowl at her suggestion. 'Cally, with that stare,

SEPARATION

you're the spit of our dear Martha! Of all the unfortunate things to run in a family.' She co-opts our mother across the room: 'Luciana dear, don't you agree? Wouldn't it be nice if your darling girls were to put on a little show?'

My mother gives an indulgent smile. 'Sure the girls'll oblige, won't you, honeys?' Her eyes settle icily on me.

'I can't sing,' I say loudly.

'Why, just about anybody but a cold and empty kettle can sing,' Great Aunt Beth replies. 'Your little sister is willing.' Etta smiles, as usual betraying my resistance to adult manipulation with her desperation to please.

The middle of the room where the casket stood is empty, the furniture still making space for it as if in expectation of its return. An arm round each of us, Great Aunt Beth guides us here, where we can be seen by my grandfather, mother and the few other relatives and friends lingering after the funeral service.

My mother lollops towards me in high heels – this is how she lives in my memory: tall, thin and thrust forward slightly, like a rearing insect, creepy but ultimately crushable. She raises a fine black eyebrow. 'Just go along with something for someone else's sake, for once in your life,' she murmurs in my ear. 'This is not about you.' She straightens and smiles at Great Aunt Beth.

Etta sings sweetly – I can't remember what. I chant, with my eyes closed, 'A sailor went to sea, sea, sea...' I run into the hall to hide my burning cheeks and brimming eyes. The porch door is open. I am about to climb on to the swing-seat when I hear: 'The world is a far, far bigger place than who's in that parlour.' My grandfather stands on the porch; his sore eyes peer at me, magnified by his half-moon glasses. 'Your grandma, she was wise to that fact, the smallness of people's parlours, and their lives. She hated those sing-a-longs. Always belly-aching at my family's ways. I reckon she saw right through them, knew baloney for what it was. Singing a plain old little ditty that none of them can possibly coo over, now that was inspired.' He chuckles, then his eyes go watery. 'She'd have been proud of you.'

He leads me to his study, a gloomy green-papered room with a worn armchair and a desk, and a TV in the corner perched on a bookcase. He puts a pale wooden box, about the size of a cereal packet, on the desk in front of me and runs his fingers over it. 'Years of polish. She never let me varnish it. She was right about that.

'Now, Calliope, your mama and grandma, they didn't always see eye to eye. I wouldn't blame your mama, after everything that happened and all, but she might figure this box ain't worth the keeping. So, you hold on to it for me, you hear? In case I get taken with no warning. That way you all get to know your grandma.'

He must have recognised how sly I was, to have had any faith that a twelve year old could not only keep something precious safe, but also hidden from adults. No one notices me slip the box into the suitcase tucked under the guest bed I share with Etta. That night, as we lie unable to sleep for the heat and jetlag, Etta puts words to the cut-time, two-note locust song that saws through the damp night air: right-wrong, right-wrong, right-wrong.

The next – and also penultimate – day of our stay, curiosity has me lingering near where Luciana sits next to a woman I do not know. 'But I really don't see how, without Martha to help him, Daddy can continue.' These are my mother's exact words: sinewy, resistant. Her cigarette holder is poised in front of her like my father with his inoculating syringe. Diamonds – probably paste but I didn't know that then – sparkle like frost against the woman's black collar. The needle of a record player is tipped with a diamond: this recently learnt fact pops into my mind. A diamond necklace playing my mother's words over and over, like a song turning in my head, like Etta's locust song. All these years later, I can barely hear the locusts, but my mother's words resonate as if she were speaking them beside me now.

Emma Rhind-Tutt is working on *Separation* and a police procedural where a police family liaison officer investigates a missing baby. In book publishing in the 1990s, she now writes full time. Her work gained special commendation for the Escalator Award in 2009 and has appeared on the app *Quick Fictions*.

JESS ROUSSOS
Borderland

*An extract from the end of chapter three of a novel
set in a South African game reserve*

MARK PARKED THE CAR SQUARELY IN THE MIDDLE OF THE TAR ROAD before the closed, locked, shut, unmanned West Gate.

The boom was down, the metal gates chained. The guardhouse was dark, and even from that distance it looked deserted. None of them spoke. Mark considered the road beyond the gate, the continuation of the road they were on, which was one and the same and yet irretrievably different. Outside the park the trees were more contained, thinned out and manicured, and the road was less dusty. It swept away to the top of a rise and disappeared from view. And as it did so he felt a version of himself, fresher, neater and more tamed, disappear from view along it.

Mark unlocked his door, but hesitated about getting out. They were in the park proper, not at a rest camp or picnic spot, and it was becoming increasingly clear to him that they had been left behind, somehow, or abandoned.

He drove as close as he could get to the gate and climbed out cautiously to confirm that it was impenetrable.

'I think we should climb over.' Shaun's voice made Mark flinch, shattering his thoughts.

Ryan grunted his assent, coming to stand behind them, his arms hanging alongside his thighs, palms turned inwards, gorilla-like.

'Fence is electric,' said Mark. He bent and broke off a long blade of grass and touched it to the fence; there was a loud tick as the current jolted through it and he felt a small bubble of electricity travel up his fingers.

'Not the gate,' said Shaun, repeating his trick, and then rapping on the gate with his knuckles.

'What's the point? That's probably a private reserve out there anyway. They're dotted all along the borders of the park. Could stretch for ages until you're properly out.'

'This is fucking bullshit.' Shaun gripped the gate in both hands. 'I am tired and hungry and I'm getting the fuck out of here.'

He watched Shaun wedge the toe of his tekkie on a crossbar and haul himself onto the gate. 'And what are you going to do when you get out? What then?' His voice rose into a shout. He felt desperate to fill the empty space around them with noise.

Shaun did not answer. He climbed further, avoiding the sharp curlicue barbs spiking out from the gate at irregular intervals. Mark watched helplessly, Ryan breathing heavily and flapping his T-shirt beside him.

Mark estimated that Shaun was three-quarters of the way up the fence when an unmistakably human and mechanical sound splintered the air: a gunshot. The noise reverberated and ricocheted off the trees and sky and Mark dropped to the dusty ground. He heard Shaun shout as he fell and then saw the dust thud up as he hit the ground.

'What the fuck – what the fuck –' He tried to stop the words from coming out of his mouth as he stared around, dragging his cheeks across the ground and searching for the source.

A voice, distorted and magnified, rang out: THAT WAS A WARNING SHOT. DO NOT ATTEMPT TO CLIMB THE GATE AGAIN.

Mark crouched shakily, staring out through the gate. He could just make out a silhouette coming into view at the top of the rise.

THIS PARK HAS BEEN QUARANTINED. DO NOT ATTEMPT TO LEAVE OR BREAK THE QUARANTINE AGAIN. THIS IS FOR YOUR OWN SAFETY. I REPEAT, DO NOT ATTEMPT TO BREACH THE PERIMETER.

Mark squinted at the figure and then scuttled sideways towards the open car door, pulling binoculars from the interior and focusing them on the silhouette.

A BUFFER ZONE HAS BEEN ESTABLISHED OUTSIDE THE PARK. ANY PERSON IN THAT BUFFER ZONE WILL BE SHOT ON SIGHT. DO NOT ATTEMPT TO BREACH THE PERIMETER.

Army fatigues sharpened into clarity as more men joined the

speaker on the rise. Mark watched as he raised the loudspeaker again. The barrel of his gun stuck up behind him.

TESTS ARE UNDERWAY. ONCE THE INCUBATION PERIOD OF THE VIRUS HAS BEEN ESTABLISHED THE PARK WILL BE DE-QUARANTINED.

The soldier turned to his companion, who had raised binoculars of his own and was studying Mark as intently as Mark was him, and consulted with him before continuing.

LEAVE THE PERIMETER IMMEDIATELY. AVOID CONTACT WITH OTHER PEOPLE.

He lowered the loudspeaker and turned away. Mark stood up and raised a hand, unsure of anything except that he didn't want to be left.

'Wait!' he shouted, immediately regretting it.

I REPEAT. MOVE AWAY FROM THE PERIMETER AND AVOID CONTACT WITH OTHER PEOPLE.

The soldier turned and, almost as an afterthought, spoke once more.

GOOD LUCK.

'What the fuck?' Mark looked at Ryan, who was crouched beside him. 'We've got to get out of here before they start shooting off more warning shots.'

Shaun groaned loudly and Mark turned to look at him, snapping his mouth shut.

'Shit, are you OK?'

'Jesus! You're fucking bleeding, dude.' Ryan was sitting in the dust; he scrambled to his feet and helped Mark pull Shaun off the ground.

'Did the shot—'

'Fucking barbed wire on the gate.' Shaun spat on the ground as Mark and Ryan sat him on the backseat of the car. Blood was spurting out of a ragged cut down the inside of his arm. Mark winced and tried not to look at it, handing him a towel from the back of the car.

'Shit, we've got to get away from here, boet. Then we can look at it.' Mark helped Shaun wrap his arm up in the towel, pulling it tight over the wound, and then ran around to the driver's seat.

'There was a lookout spot a little way back,' suggested Ryan.

Mark drove flat out, the car flying over the bumps in the road, Shaun groaning and swearing. He turned into the lookout point and parked. Ryan helped Shaun sit up in the back seat with his legs outside of the car and his injured arm on his lap.

'Let's take a look,' said Ryan, kneeling in front of Shaun and nodding at Mark to do the same.

Mark rotated the injured arm gently and felt his torso ripple in a heave as he looked at the wound.

He turned his head and swallowed, and then turned back to Shaun to examine the tear. Shaun's inner left arm was ripped. There was a long gash about ten centimetres long between wrist and elbow, the skin flapping outwards and blood still pumping sluggishly out. Ryan pressed down hard on it with the towel and gestured for Mark to raise it higher into the air. With the wound cleared of excess blood, Mark could see through to layers of flesh and muscle. It was quite deep in one spot, and there were several other, shallower tears around the main wound.

'How, how bad is it?' Shaun's face was completely white and Mark thought that all the blood in his head must be draining out of his arm.

'It probably needs stitches,' said Ryan calmly, 'but I think you were actually lucky, it's not bleeding *that* much, so I think you missed nicking major veins or arteries.'

Mark gaped at Ryan as he continued to pat at the wound gently, mopping up the blood.

'My mom's a nurse, remember,' Ryan said, and Mark nodded. 'Can you grab the plasters? They'll have to do.'

Mark ran around to the boot and felt relief wash over him as he found the packet with the plasters and Savlon disinfectant liquid. He walked back around the car and held them out to Ryan, whose bulk now seemed authoritative and reassuring – he had somehow drawn his stomach up into his chest. Ryan held Shaun's arm in the air with the towel wrapped around it and Mark was for the first time incredibly glad that his brother-in-law was there.

'Dilute some of that Savlon, will you, so we can wash it. Shaun, hold the towel on and keep it in the air, dude.'

Mark did as he was told, placing the cooler box lid upside down on the ground beside Shaun. He filled the shallow vessel with water and mixed in about half of the small bottle of Savlon, stopping at Ryan's 'Not too much.'

Ryan was laying out the plasters, tutting over the poor selection. They were at least the fabric kind, which seemed more medical to Mark than the plastic ones with dinosaurs that he had always had as a child.

'Remember monkey's blood and the dinosaur plasters?' He looked at Shaun, who had his eyes closed and his arms raised above his head. Shaun smiled and nodded, not opening his eyes. Ryan lowered Shaun's arm and peeled off the towel, which had gone from a dirty grey to a bright red. The seeping blood had slowed, and the wound was even more worrying now that it was unobscured. Mark stared at it, fixated by the anatomy on show, the layers of fat and skin and muscle visible in the deepest part of the gash; he leaned in closer, focusing on a flap of already shrivelled skin that reminded him of the slimy uncooked chicken skin on a drumstick.

'Hold his arm still so I can wash it.' Ryan snapped his fingers in front of Mark's face and Mark shook his head and then gripped Shaun's hand and elbow awkwardly, his fingers slipping, unsure where to hold.

Ryan splashed some of the diluted antiseptic over the wound and Shaun groaned and twisted; Mark tightened his grip and noticed beads of sweat forming along his friend's receding hairline. Ryan washed the arm again and then towelled it off. He ran his hands through the remainder of the antiseptic, scrubbing them together to get them clean, and then grimaced and began to try to close the wound. He pushed the flesh back into its original place, laying the torn skin over it, pinching the flapping lips of the tear shut. All the while blood continued to pump out in time with Shaun's heartbeat, which Mark could feel in the crook of his elbow. Once Ryan had laid the bits of flesh roughly back in place, a grisly jigsaw with the pieces lined up but not clicked together, he began to select plasters. He picked the long thin ones, which could reach across the wound.

'Shaun, hold it still now, buddy. I need Mark to help me with these Band-Aids.' Ryan looked at him and he nodded, releasing

Shaun's arm. They peeled off the backings of the plasters and Mark watched Ryan demonstrate with the first one, closest to the elbow. He placed one end of it on Shaun's unbroken skin and then stretched it across, pinching the wound closed with his other hand and laying it down on the other side. Mark started at the wrist and they worked steadily, using up three quarters of the box of plasters, laying them as close together as possible until they had covered the entire rip with sticky fabric. Ryan shredded the towel into strips and wound them around Shaun's arm to finish.

'It's gonna be a bitch coming off, but it'll do for now.'

Jess Roussos is from Jo'burg, South Africa. She now lives in London, and is currently working on her first novel. *Borderland* is post-apocalyptic fiction in the absence of apocalypse. It explores the fragility of societal rules and the lengths we will go to in order to survive.

ANEALLA SAFDAR

Number One

An extract

SEEMA FORGOT ABOUT THE CHAPATI TOASTING ON THE SKILLET UNTIL IT BURNT and set off the smoke alarm. It was teatime, but since Latif had delivered his suggestion in the morning, his breath still sour from sleep, she hadn't been able to concentrate on much. She knew he was waiting for a sign from her that she was all right with it, and would be by his side, and so she'd found ways to avoid him. She had taken a long bath and made several unneeded trips to the loo, vacuumed the stairs barely coated in a day's layer of dust, and performed extra verses and devotions for each of her prayers.

'Everything OK in there?' he called from the sitting room. There was a hesitance in his voice, a little extra concern, as though he were responsible for the shrill, ringing sound.

'Fine,' she shouted, matter-of-fact. 'I'll be in in a minute.'

She turned the cooker off and opened a window. Looking out at their square lawn, she remembered, not for the first time that day, the weekend that they'd viewed the house ten years ago, when it was a new build. Latif had come into some inheritance and his cab company was doing well. When the estate agent had shown them the kitchen, the room now choking, she'd said to Seema, 'Great isn't it? Just the right size for two,' and whispered in her ear, 'or three.' Seema smiled at the time. She'd been thirty-three then, when her hair was thick and swooped to her navel, when she had her *salwar kameez* tailored in the latest fashions, when there'd still been a glint of hope for an 'or three'.

Outside in the thin spray of rain, she scattered the singed remains of flatbread for the birds in between the washing line and

NUMBER ONE

herb patch where coriander and mint grew. Recently, she'd spent more time planting flowers and plucking weeds, and was proud that the garden finally looked as immaculate as indoors. As she admired a row of hydrangeas, she vowed to herself that whatever would change from here, she'd put her foot down on one thing: they would not move from their beloved three-bedroomed home in Pleasington, in the posh part of Blackburn. On this condition, she'd accept that a second wife would soon be living with them, a much younger woman than her, one able to bear Latif his first child, and preferably a son at that.

By the time she went back inside, the alarm had stopped. She took a tray of food to Latif and nodded at him once. It was enough to let him know that she had conceded.

'I was sure you weren't going to disappoint me *Jaan*,' he said, and ate a bite of spiced chicken and spinach. 'You're right to get on board with this. It'll give us a much-needed boost, perk things up a bit, eh?'

She rolled her eyes. It had been a while since he last *jaaned* her. 'If it's what you really want,' she said. 'But we're not moving house.'

'Why would we? Big enough for everyone here.'

'Let's hope so.'

'You're a good woman, Seems. The best there is out there. I mean, if you could have had kids, we wouldn't really be going through all of this.'

She put her forearm over her stomach as if to protect her womb from hearing.

'I know, I know, it's not your fault. It's God's will, isn't it? If this is how we're meant to get a son, then this is how it will be.'

Usually she'd agree on the point about the will of God. It was something she'd comforted him with many times before. But instead she said, 'I'll make us a cup of tea,' and left, her shoulders sagging with defeat. As soon as her back was turned, he switched the television on to the cricket.

Back at the hob, she poured milk into a saucepan with teabags and sugar, put it over a high heat, and leaned on the fridge wondering where they'd find this new wife.

If it was left to Latif, he'd suggest going to Pakistan and he'd want to take her with him. In their twenty-six years together since their traditionally arranged marriage, they'd not been apart for more than a day, out of custom and habit. He'd probably spend months in his native village, chest puffed like a feudal lord spoiling what was left of his family in the Punjab with gifts and money until one of them swindled him. She pictured a cousin or uncle offering up a scrawny dairymaid they knew for the price of a car or a ticket to England. He tended to be naive with those who deserved distrust, and vice versa.

She shivered, shook her head, and stirred slowly. Things had changed since they visited the mountains of Murree for their honeymoon, that first and last trip back to the country they'd left as toddlers. Muggings at gunpoint, violence in the streets, harassment in the bazaars, they were all on the rise. That's what sister Uzma from the local mosque had told her. A woman from Pakistan might end up being dishonest. Then again, what if she wasn't? If she was truthful and beautiful and young and slim, they'd have a whole cricket team's worth of children and never return to Blackburn. Seema would live and die in the shadow of her husband and his new perfect partner, in a land she no longer recognised or cared much for, a place she was almost sure felt the same about her.

She crushed a cardamom pod between her back teeth, threw it into the bubbling chai, and decided that she'd have to get right 'on board' as Latif had said. She needed someone impartial to talk to, who wouldn't judge her or ask questions, someone who had answers. No, she didn't need someone. People were never neutral. She needed something. She'd have to search on the internet.

'Seems, what's taking so long? Bring us a biscuit too would you?' Latif hollered over the commentary.

The tea was stewed. Like the chapati it had remained over the flame for too long, but she would serve it anyway.

Bunched up on the sofa they slurped together, him from a saucer, her from a cup. It was like any other evening, as if nothing had happened. He caressed the end of her scarf between his fingertips, and she rubbed a little almond oil on his bald patch. But when an advert interrupted the Test Match, she took the remote and hit standby.

NUMBER ONE

'So what are we looking for?' she said, and they decided awkwardly and quickly, like the conversation was causing them both pain, that Latif's second wife should be childless, between twenty-five and thirty, and able to hold conversation in English. They would consider divorcees and women without both parents, but not daughters of widows. They knew too well the burden a lonely mother could weigh, since Seema's father had passed.

Once it was over, Latif reached for the last chocolate bourbon. 'And if she takes more than two samosas in one sitting, we'll have to say no. If she can't look after herself, how will she be able to look after me?' he said, and patted his round belly.

Seema's laugh surprised them both. 'I thought this was about you getting a son, an heir to Latif's Limousines, not losing weight or getting some nookie you old fool.'

'Don't worry, love. You'll always be my number one.' He pinched the loyal flesh surrounding her hips. 'It's always going to be you. Only you.'

'Right.' She returned his hand. 'And where do we plan to find number two?'

Latif chewed his bottom lip and in that same hesitant voice said, 'Pakistan?'

One afternoon a week later in the spare room, Seema found Latif's Glenfiddich nestled between splintered cricket bats and her old treadle sewing machine. She sat on the carpet against the radiator, legs stretched out with the laptop on her thighs, and took a swig. Usually she only drank to relieve a cold, but this time it was for courage. Emboldened by the whisky, she prised the computer open, closed the windows she'd viewed over the past seven days – music clips of lovelorn ghazals, scanned photos of them as happy newlyweds in seaside towns from Blackpool to Margate – and started tapping questions into Yahoo:

What's the oldest age a woman can get pregnant? When can men stop having children? Why does my fifty-four-year-old husband want to be younger? Can the evil eye make you barren?

And with a second sip:

How can I be sure my husband won't want to divorce me and live with his other woman? Where to look for my husband's second wife?

The second wife search threw up pages bursting with religious advice. Virtual imams surfed across message boards, replying to hoards of women panicked by the fear of being usurped. The scholars preached on forums, urging jealousies to be put aside in the name of sisterhood and the understanding that men, by their very nature, are polygamous. There were stories about husbands who didn't tell their first wives before indulging in another. Perhaps Seema was luckier than she felt. Other tales, though in the minority, were of women shunned by their first husbands through affairs or abuse, and accepted by a second. There were none, and this disappointed her, about women taking on two husbands in the same way. She knew it wasn't necessarily allowed, but she'd have liked to have read about it nevertheless.

Really what she was after though, was a stranger, a physical intermediary, to oversee the process. She was too bitter to look by herself and yet unable to leave it to Latif. Mementoes of his impulsive decision-making were everywhere. Unused gadgets in the garage, boxes of never-opened flatpack furniture in the loft, and even a car or two in his fleet of taxis that he no longer wanted, having bid for them excitedly at auctions.

Back on the index, she tried to make her search more specific:

Marriage agents to help first wife find second wife for British Pakistani husband. Pakistani marriage agents for Pakistani second wives but not located in dangerous Pakistan. Marriage agents in...

Pausing to think, she took her hands away from the keyboard and looked to the ceiling for ideas.

When she fixed her eyes back on the screen, the search engine had completed the rest of the field for her.

Marriage agents in Dubai.

A link at the top of the page was promoted: *Dubai's Desi Solutions.* It was a company running from the Emirates which catered to her dilemma.

She clicked it twice, and was led to a questionnaire which she completed, ticking the couple's preferences for age, height, weight, skin tone, marital history, family history, and mental history. For the first time in a week, she felt a pang of guilt. She was online shopping for a child-bearer, someone whose sole purpose would be to breed. She was no better than a farmer.

NUMBER ONE

She hit send and made a prayer that the form would get muddled in electronic waves.

Anealla Safdar is working on a novel and short story collection. Last September, she returned to England from a five-year dance with words in Qatar and the UAE, where she was a journalist at Al Jazeera and *The National* newspaper. She is the recipient of the Seth Donaldson Memorial Trust Bursary.

POPPY SEBAG-MONTEFIORE

Listeners

Extract from a novel

Wang Yao and Sun Hai have been married for thirty-five years. They are being relocated from their home to a new living development on the outskirts of the city. They found a loophole stating that divorcees can apply for a new flat each.

WANG YAO TOLD SUN HAI NOT TO DISCUSS THEIR DIVORCE WITH THE NEIGHBOURS. She returned to their building and he joined the crowd around the chess game on the stone bench outside building number six. The unbeaten neighbourhood champion was playing against a newcomer who, with strategy and determination, had been moving in on him over the summer. Each game they played now was an exciting one, and some of the residents had bets down. The neighbours leaned upon one another, almost propping each other up, and Sun Hai squeezed in and found himself a place. Each player held a piece that he had seized from the other, which they tapped on the chessboard while they scanned the board for danger and planned their next moves. A rhythm emerged between them that hypnotised the crowd.
   Tap
                Dat
   Tap
                Dat
  Sun Hai became distracted when he saw Old Fa and his wife, who he and Wang Yao had tried to hide from at the divorce bureau that morning. Old Fa's wife returned to their building and Old Fa came over towards Sun Hai.

LISTENERS

'We got married when we were too young and divorced when we were too old,' Old Fa said to him as he slipped himself into the audience next to Sun Hai.

Sun Hai looked at Old Fa, then back to the game. They stood, held together by the crowd. The players passed the game between one another. Some of the onlookers were calling out advice to the current champion.

'Let's go out for a drink,' Old Fa said.

Sun Hai nodded and they dislodged themselves from the group.

Sun Hai knew it was wrong whichever way he looked at it. He knew that many other men would disagree, or wouldn't even attend to the question. But if this was ever to be, and usually it was never to be, it was to be now. He and Wang Yao were digesting, they hadn't yet talked it over; they were divorced. This had been her idea. She'd done this. And this was what men did, what they had always done. Men went out into the world and did brave things, and they'd bring the fruits, or whatever they'd learnt, back to the home. Sun Hai knew what he wanted to do. His body needed to. After sharing a small bottle of rice wine, Old Fa and Sun Hai discussed going north, to the university district, where things were cheap, but they realised that the usual clientele there would be much younger, and that would be embarrassing. They didn't even think of going east, into the business district, where prices would be high. South they'd ruled out, because it was too poor down there, and so probably not clean, they thought, and it wasn't worth risking disease or infection to save a few pennies. And west, well, west was too residential and undeveloped. They doubted there would be much there. Outside the small white tiled restaurant where they drank, eight lanes of traffic inched past them in both directions. They decided to walk a little to the northeast, to the entertainment district.

Sun Hai and Old Fa sat in barber's chairs. They'd chosen this place because it looked clean and smart and because it was empty, apart from a group of girls sitting on the sofa near the shop window, waiting. Sun Hai and Old Fa were still the only two customers by the time their head massage had finished. A lady with a name badge saying Cindy on it massaged Sun Hai's head.

She seemed to be the boss of the place, probably in her thirties. A slightly younger woman massaged the back of Fa's shoulders. Sun Hai now saw, through the reflection in his mirror, that the other two girls behind him on the sofa were children, perhaps around ten years old. They were playing a card game together. Cindy took out a hairbrush and a pair of scissors.

'Would you like a haircut today, sir?'

'I won't have a haircut,' he said.

'Would you like any other treatments?'

'What kind of treatments do you have?' Sun Hai looked across at Old Fa. Old Fa gave him an encouraging nod. Sun Hai wished that he would be shown a list, from which he could choose whatever sounded good.

'We have the full body massage,' Cindy said, and that seemed to be all.

'We'll have two of those,' Sun Hai said, and checked with Old Fa, who nodded to Sun Hai and to the girl who was massaging his own head.

The two masseuses showed Sun Hai and Old Fa into a back corridor. Cindy turned to Sun Hai.

'A high bed or a low bed?'

'A high bed,' Sun Hai said. Old Fa looked disappointed. The girls led them into two adjacent slim booth-like rooms.

'Take off your clothes and lie up here, and I will be back in a moment,' Cindy said to Sun Hai. 'Would you like a cup of tea?'

'OK.'

Sun Hai took his trousers off, and then his underpants. He folded them on the back of a chair. The area behind the shop-front looked like it doubled up as a home. He'd seen a kitchen and a bathroom along the corridor. He held one leg in the air, stretched and bent it, and then did the same with the other leg. He took off his T-shirt, then got up onto the massage bed and lay on his back. He wondered how many people lived back here and where they slept. Cindy returned and handed him a paper cup of jasmine tea. She turned on a CD playing Chinese pipe music and turned down the lights. Sun Hai kept all expression from his face, but what he felt was pleasure.

'What?' Cindy called out, startling Sun Hai.

LISTENERS

In the dimmed light he saw her turn her head over her shoulder and listen to something outside the room. She rested one hand on Sun Hai's navel and with the other, she stretched to turn down the music.

'Mum,' came the voice of the young girl, 'we're going out to buy some ice lollies.'

'That's fine,' Cindy called out over her shoulder. The shop door banged. Cindy turned the music back up and returned to Sun Hai.

He closed his eyes.

Usually Sun Hai showered, but he'd hurried back home to get in the bath before Wang Yao came home from her dancing. He sat by the taps, his face hidden, enjoying the steam from a flannel when Wang Yao entered the bathroom. He tensed. Without speaking, she took off her trousers, shirt, bra, popsocks and knickers and put herself into the bath with Sun Hai. There they both sat, side by side, backs to the wall, facing the centre of the room, their legs crossed.

'You're back early. What happened to the dancing?' He dunked the flannel in the water in front of him, twirled it, and began to rub it up and down the side of his arm.

Without answering, Wang Yao reached for her white flannel, soaked it and wrung it out. She put her hand on Sun Hai's far shoulder, pulled it towards her, and swivelled herself around so she was sitting behind him. She raised one knee above the water, rested on the heel of her other foot and scrubbed his back. She soaked the flannel again, scrunched it in her hand, then stretched it out and stroked it down the sides of Sun Hai's neck. She took a corner of the flannel to his ear. She brought the front of his torso back round to face her and rubbed in circles under his arms, then washed the front of his chest, beneath his pectoral muscles, along the lines of his collarbone to his other ear and down his arms to his hands.

'Pass your foot to me.' She nodded towards it, under his calf.

'No need,' he said.

'Don't worry, give it to me.'

'I'm swimming early in the morning. It's time to go to bed.'

POPPY SEBAG-MONTEFIORE

Sun Hai stepped out of the bath. Wang Yao watched him wrap a towel around his bottom and leave the room. She stood. Drops of water meandered down her thighs.

In their bedroom, orange rinds curled as they dried on the windowsill. They'd have to collect those in the morning; no more tasks, or tidying could be attempted that day. Sun Hai took out the bamboo mat and placed it on the floor by the bed.

'Why are you using that?'

'Just because,' Sun Hai said.

He lowered himself onto the mat. She lay on their bed. As silence began to establish itself she rolled over to the side of the bed, dangled her arm and tapped Sun Hai. He made no move.

'This wasn't well thought out,' she said.

Poppy Sebag-Montefiore worked as a journalist for the BBC, and was the Channel 4 News China correspondent before they had a bureau there. She speaks fluent Mandarin. She was awarded the Malcolm Bradbury Scholarship to study an MA in Creative Writing at UEA. She's now at work on her first novel.

NICK SHADOWEN

The Old Sea Dog

NICK CHARLEY DIDN'T LIKE HIS DAUGHTER'S FIANCÉ MUCH. He knew it the second he shook his limp, damp hand. Nick often made quick judgements about people and his judgements often proved to be right. He didn't see why this time should be any different.

But Laurel Lake was blue and beautiful underneath the late morning sun and Nick told himself to keep his mouth shut. He told himself he'd catch a damn big fish and be nice to the kid for his daughter's sake. Scratching the stubble on his chin, he looked at her standing there along the bank, raising her hand above her eyes as she looked out across the lake to the tree-lined shore on the other side.

A slight breeze trickled through the pine trees near the water's edge and Nick closed his eyes and breathed deeply. The grass was damp from last night's rain and he liked the smell and he always fished well in the morning after a rain. He looked at his daughter again as she and her mother began feeding pieces of bread crust from the picnic basket to a duckling that had climbed the bank by itself in search of food.

Yes, thought Nick, it is a good day to fish. He reached into the back of the pickup and took out the wooden tackle box and handed it to the boy standing before him.

'Heavy,' said the boy, bending his knees to set it on the ground.

Nick said nothing. If this kid made his little girl happy that was fine with him. He pulled his cap lower over his eyes to keep out the sun and opened the can of bait and began threading a worm onto his hook.

THE OLD SEA DOG

'Know how to hook a worm?' Nick asked.

'Yes, sir,' said the boy.

Nick handed him the other rods and they hooked the worms in silence as the breeze picked up off the lake.

'Say,' said the boy after a moment, as if he'd been searching for the words, 'You hear what Nixon did? That rat...'

Nick had heard about it that morning on the radio and it meant nothing to him. He looked down toward the dock at the two women chatting and glancing back at them. He reminded himself to be nice.

'No wonder this country's in a pickle,' the boy was saying, 'Our boys over in 'Nam killing innocent children and—'

'You missed the draft, then?'

The boy paused for a second and then finished hooking the worm. He smiled and looked down at his shoes.

'I'm a student,' he said, 'at Penn.'

Nick Charley unfastened the ties and then took one end of the canoe and motioned to the boy to take the other. They lowered it from the roof of the truck and began walking it down to the water's edge.

'Exactly thirty years ago,' Nick said, 'at the age of twenty, I joined the United States Navy. I didn't want to get one of them letters, you know, one of them letters that said *I Want You*.'

The boy smiled politely.

Nick continued. 'They made me an officer, not sure why, maybe because I had some education, could spell my name and count to ten.'

The young woman came up and put her arms around her fiancé. 'Oh you're not telling war stories again are you, Daddy?'

The wife brought the life vests from the truck and put them aboard and then Nick and the boy slid the big canoe into the lake. Nick stood there for a moment watching the ripples move across the smooth surface. Then he turned to the boy.

'Yes sir, I'm an old sailor. An old sea dog. They checked my eyes, ears, and ass and then sent me to the Pacific,' Nick said, 'To fight the Japs.'

His wife rolled her eyes but he paid her no mind.

'When I reached the base at Guam I already had Cat Fever, got it stationed in Frisco. You know what Cat Fever is?'

The boy said he didn't.

'Caught it stationed in Frisco. Then I reported to headquarters in the Pacific, this officer of twenty, walking down the red goddamn carpet with just my suitcase in one hand and my balls in the other. I told 'em, "Nicholas Charley reporting for duty." They looked at me and said I was early and to come back tomorrow. So I'm walking out, down this fancy red carpet, and guess who's coming towards me.'

The wife and daughter looked at each other and sighed and then the boy asked, 'Who?'

'Nimitz and Halsey,' said Nick.

'What did you do?' asked the boy.

'What the hell you think I did? I got my ass off the carpet, dropped my suitcase, and saluted. They were probably askin' themselves what the sam hell the Navy had come to, a twenty-year-old officer. It's a damn wonder we didn't lose the war.'

'That's a nice story, dear,' said the wife, 'Now let's finish putting these things in the boat.'

The boy tied the canoe off to a tree while they loaded the reels and picnic basket and tackle box. But Nick Charley wasn't done with his story.

'Clear as day I remember it,' he said, scratching his stubble again.

'What's that, sir?' asked the boy.

'Daddy...' said the daughter.

Nick looked at the young man whom he did not like. 'The day the war ended, of course. I was second in command on the ship, it was an envoy ship... You know what an envoy ship is?'

'No, sir,' the boy said.

'Envoy ship goes ahead of the battleships, guards the flanks and takes care of any Jap submarines or mines. Second in command on a goddamn battleship envoy, twenty years old. I was the gunnery officer and didn't know a goddamn thing about 'em, couldn't even shoot one myself, come to think of it. I tell you honest I don't know how we won that war.'

'You were saying about the war's end, dear...' the wife said. They were all in the canoe, waiting to push off, and the sun was getting hot.

THE OLD SEA DOG

Nick brought the paddles up and handed one to the boy at the other end of the canoe.

'Well, I was inside the control room on the radio and the news came in from HQ. They said it just like that, all matter of fact. "The war's over." I put the radio down for a second and then picked it back up and said back to them, "Are you shittin' me?" They said "No sir." I put the radio down and went out onto the deck into the sunlight. The men were all sweating and some had taken their shirts off. It was a real hot day with no breeze. We'd been out there for almost two years. Like I said, I was only second in command but I clasped my hands round my mouth and hollered, "Now hear this, now hear this, the war is over. I repeat, the war is over."'

Nick Charley looked at his wife and she looked back at him fondly.

'Now the captain,' he continued, 'was none too happy about me making that announcement to the crew before I reported it to him. But we were good pals, he and I, and I just looked him square in the eye and said, "Goddamnit Bill, everyone on this ship deserves to know at the same time."'

The boy looked at him and said, 'That's some story.'

'Now let's go fishing,' said Nick, and he shoved them off from the bank with the paddle. But the canoe didn't go anywhere.

'What the hell you doin' back there,' said Nick, 'Row.'

'I am,' said the boy, and he began rowing even harder. But still the canoe didn't move.

'Jesus H Christ,' said Nick, 'Hand me the damn paddle.'

The boy handed him the paddle and Nick swiped it down forcefully into the glassy water. But still the canoe remained where it was.

Then the wife spoke. 'I think we're still tied to the tree, dear.'

The daughter laughed, and then the wife, and then the boy.

For the rest of the day, the wife from time to time looked at Nick Charley and gave him a mock salute.

'Aww, what the hell you doin',' he said finally.

'Nothing,' said the wife, 'Just salutin' an old sailor. An old sea dog.'

And they all laughed. Except for Nick Charley. He fished steadily and quietly that day and though the others caught nothing, by sunset he had filled his cooler with five largemouth bass, each nearly two feet long.

Nick Shadowen studied philosophy at Duquesne University where he received the Undergraduate Award for Excellence in Philosophy. He has travelled throughout Europe and America, living for a time in Rome and Mount Desert Island, Maine, where he finished his first novel. He is currently working on a book of interlinked tales about courage, choice, exile, and art.

SOPHIA VELTFORT

Gus and Diane

Excerpt of a short story

BIKRAM WAS CANCELLED, THE SIGN SAID, APOLOGIES. There was nothing to be done, Gus saw. A lesser man might have broken down.

He must've been sitting on the bench for about ten minutes when the door from the stairs opened, and a handful of middle-aged men and women in sweats and T-shirts trickled through the hall to the studio across from his, which had always been empty when he'd gotten here for his 5:15. They looked awkward and sorrowful, like understudy souls who'd never expected to be called.

Gus followed them into the studio. A short, dumpy instructress with sandy-grey hair stood by the mirrors.

'Excuse me, ma'am,' he said. 'What class is this?'

'We're the Tai Chi Society, New York Branch.' She looked mildly affronted.

'I usually do Bikram across the hall,' he explained, gesturing vaguely over his shoulder. 'But it's cancelled. I don't suppose I could try–ah–Tai Chi?'

She appraised him, shrugged. 'It's an intermediate class, so you might get lost, but you can follow the class in the mirrors, and I'll be up front. Ten bucks for a drop-in.'

He pulled out his wallet, handed her a ten.

She pocketed it. 'Pleasure to have you. Find a spot anywhere you like.'

Gus moved to the back of the studio. He bent to touch his toes. Upside down, he saw a willowy woman with long dark hair and froggish eyes enter the studio. Her tight black leggings suggested

GUS AND DIANE

toned legs. Behind her stood a teenage girl so like her, Gus had to assume it was her daughter. The willowy woman's eyes met his between his knees.

Diane's miscalculation grew more evident with each passing moment. Her Tai Chiers were dingy and moth-eaten, overlooked and beaten-down. She had sensed this before but never seen it so clearly, reflected in the gentle disdain coloring Francesca's face. Diane blushed for their outmoded clothing, their loneliness, the way they sucked at their classmates for some sense of community before returning to empty apartments and cheap takeout dinners for one. It was clear that her daughter saw this and felt sorry for her, looked at her in surprise but not disbelief.

But the class was starting. Diane saw no way of sending Frannie away. There was nothing she could do but watch the scene seep outward like a stain. Nor could she stand still, now that the class had begun its set of danyus. The stupid squats only condemned her more.

The teacher was announcing the break. Time had passed. A vague recollection of sitting at her desk, imagining how she would introduce Frannie to Elaine, to Sandra, and to Bob plucked at Diane. She had envisioned each of the encounters, how each set of eyes would light up with their vision of Frannie. She made herself walk over to Frannie's chair, but she couldn't meet her eyes. Diane could sense the others hanging back.

But Bob, the oldest in the group, was ambling over. It had been Bob to whom she'd shown Frannie's picture last week. He'd told her about his grandson's cello lessons, and she told him how Frannie kept everything going at the school paper. You should see the way she has these senior boys running errands, she'd told him; Frannie could make tigers dance.

'Is this the famous Francesca?' Bob held out his hand. 'Robert Deutsch. A pleasure finally to meet you. You should hear the way your mother talks. She's so proud.'

Francesca shook his hand. 'Nice to meet you.' Her lips curved into the form of a smile.

Bob seemed uncertain how to proceed. 'Well, I'd better go get some water. Have to hydrate these old bones.' He patted his hands against his slender ribcage. 'See you around.' The floor creaked steadily beneath his retreating tennis shoes.

'It'll be pretty much the same for the rest of the class,' Diane said to Frannie's knees. 'Why don't I catch you at home?'

'Didn't you want me to meet people?'

'You saw Bob. Most of the others I wanted you to meet aren't here today,' she lied. 'I should've checked. They'll be so jealous when they hear Bob got to see you while they weren't around.'

'OK,' Frannie said. She picked up her bag and coat, gave a last glance at the room, and left.

It had been bad, no doubt about that. Gus had been there only thirty minutes and already he could see how the girl's presence had dampened the class.

He found the willowy woman sitting on the bench in the hall. Her head leaned against the wall, her eyes on the ceiling. He sat down.

'Kids these days,' he found himself blurting. 'I once brought my son to Bikram. Still haven't lived it down.' That was a complete lie. Liam had loved it. He'd been impressed with Gus's tree pose. Everyone had loved Liam.

She turned to look at him with her sad frog eyes. They were somehow very beautiful. He imagined seeing them wake up in the morning, in bed beside him, or flickering beneath their lids as they darted in dreams. He wanted to buoy them. Was that a transgression? He wasn't sure, but he didn't see how it should be. It was basic human decency. Licking a fellow traveler's wounds. But he realized he'd embarrassed her, by letting her know he'd witnessed her shame.

'How old's your son?' Her voice was lilting.

'Sixteen. Just started looking at colleges. It's a nightmare.'

The woman smiled. 'Francesca – that's my daughter – she's fifteen. I guess college is already lurking for us, too.' All of a sudden, she threw her palms to her face and moaned. 'God, that was terrible! Could everyone tell?'

'Could've been worse.' He hoped she wouldn't ask him how. He wanted to buy her a drink or a hotdog, no funny business. She felt somehow familiar, in a déjà vu sort of way, déjà connue. They were old shoes together, an acquaintance away from old friends.

GUS AND DIANE

People were filing back into the studio. Break had ended. Neither of them moved.

'I can't go back in there,' she said, flatly. 'But you should go.'

He shrugged. She was right, obviously. But he didn't want to. Anyway the studio door was closing. So he stayed, and he hoped she would, too.

'Sometimes I'll dream I have some incurable illness,' he found himself saying this time, 'something really horrible, zero hope. I'll be so devastated in the dream, the closer I circle the drain. I'll be angry, wronged. Suddenly I'll have a will to live I never even suspected. Then, just when it's been made triply clear that I'm a goner, I'll wake up. I'll be completely sweat-soaked, my pillow wet with drool and tears, my heart racing. I'll really have to pee, and I'll know I'm alive. That ever happen to you?'

'Not like that,' she said. 'But I'll dream that I'm old and on my deathbed. I'll know I've got only a couple more days, maybe hours. And I'll realize I've done it all wrong. I've lived too tentatively, cautiously, had more to regret missing than repent having done. I'll kick myself, rail against my earlier selves. Then I'll wake up, and I won't be there anymore. I'll be in my own bed.' She shrugged. 'I've had that dream since college. It gets more depressing every year.'

'I haven't had that one, yet,' he said. 'I'm probably too impulsive. Though maybe not. What's the craziest thing you've ever done?'

She looked at him like he'd touched her. He made sure his leg was far enough away, but he kept his eyes on hers. 'I guess having Frannie. I didn't like any of the men in my life, but I wanted a baby, and I knew it'd only get harder later on. So I went to a doctor, picked a donor, started saving money for her college education, built a crib.' She shrugged. 'Sometimes I worry it was selfish.'

'What's selfish about that?'

'It was all about me. I do the best I can for her, but sometimes it feels inadequate. I don't know.'

'That's ridiculous. Your daughter got one hell of a hand.'

She laughed, trying to make light of it, but her eyes glossed up. 'That's charitable of you. Of course you don't have any idea what you're talking about, but it's nice to hear, all the same. I hope she feels something similar.'

'She'd be crazy not to.'

'Huh. Well, what about you? Isn't it your turn to divulge?'

He felt like he was in college, passing a beer back and forth with a girl at a party, each of them disclosing a tidbit of personal information with each sip, enjoying the buzz and the way their lips played tag on the metal lid.

The affair with Erica was not his craziest thing. She was his biggest cruelty, his only crime. But she was just the person who had stepped forward and recognized him as the person he'd almost forgotten. She thought he was funny and sexy and looked forward to seeing him. The surprise had been vertiginous. He hadn't lusted for Erica. He just hadn't been sure he'd be able to sustain that version of himself on his own.

'I got an indoor snow machine once. We were living in San Diego and it was Christmas, no snow. I thought it'd be funny. My wife almost asked for a divorce.'

'That's your craziest thing? I expected more.'

'That's refreshing. Most folks have stopped expecting anything from me at all.' He frowned.

'I can't imagine that's true.'

'Can't you? Think about your deathbed scenario, or my illness one. Some subconscious part of ourselves delivers up these wake-up calls, these little slaps in the face, and we do wake up, we think gee, what a dream. But then what? Do we change anything? We maybe think our cereal tastes extra nice in the morning. But then we go on, carefully plodding along in the same trajectory. I don't know. Don't mind me. I just don't know.'

'But what to do? I illustrate children's books for a living. I do cereal boxes now and then to make some extra cash and buy my daughter nice clothes. I have my plants, my fish tank. I hate fish, but the building won't allow pets, and I can't afford to move anywhere that does. I try to give my daughter a good life. I read, watch movies, go to museums. When I can, I travel. I try to understand what's going on in the world.'

'What about friends, people?'

'I see people when I can. Most of my old friends live elsewhere. I like some of Frannie's friends' parents, but we don't always hit it off. Sometimes seeing them just leaves me low.'

He wanted to ask about love but worried that'd be too much. 'I like to think if I knew what to do, I'd do it, but I'm not even sure I would.'

'What do you mean?'

'My favorite part of the day is eating breakfast. Smushing avocado on toast, covering it with a boiled egg. I eat it with my hands. But then it's done, and you've got a whole day till you can do it again.'

'Try it with lemon sometimes. Gives it an extra oomph. Plus vitamin C.'

He looked at her. 'I'll try that tomorrow.'

'I'll have it, too.' She blushed. 'I guess I'd better be going. Can't hide here all day.' She fumbled for her bag, got up. 'It was nice talking to you—'

'Gus,' he said.

'Diane.' She held out her hand, and he clasped it, let it go.

Sophia Veltfort, from New York City, is a 2012 graduate from Yale and a Marshall Scholar. Her writing has been published in the *Harvard Review*, selected as a notable essay in *The Best American Essays 2013*, and performed at the Barbican. She is working on a collection of short stories.

CRAIG WARNER

The Joneses

An extract

I DON'T KNOW WHEN LUNCH BECAME SO IMPORTANT TO ME. I've never missed a meal. I've never gone hungry. And yet, at some point, lunch became everything.

When I look back, it was probably a lunch Stan Larkin bragged about that first got my attention. 'You'll never believe it,' he said. 'My lunch came and it was half a roast chicken – *half* – and it was on fire!'

'It came – what – out of the blue? You didn't order the chicken?'

'No no no, I ordered the chicken. But I didn't know it would be *half* a chicken. I thought it would be... you know... a breaded breast or something with a slice of lemon beside it. That's the sort of thing you expect when you're ordering chicken. You don't think half a fucking chicken is going to turn up at your table, and you definitely don't think it's going to be on fire!'

'Why was it on fire?'

'Because it was *flambé*!'

'Did you have to blow it out?'

'No no no, it just goes out of its own accord. It only flames for a minute.' Stan sat back, watching me, seemingly annoyed that I didn't know how things worked in the world. 'Anyway, I saw the check when they put it on our table. It was over a hundred bucks. I guess that's how much it costs to have lunch at Faust.' Stan jammed his fork into a pile of mashed potato, dipped the forkful of mashed potato into his peas, which clung to it, and shoveled it all into his mouth.

'The thing is,' he went on, in case I couldn't add up, 'that when you're represented by Jimmy Schwartz, people take you seriously.'

THE JONESES

They buy you lunch. And they show their love for you with the lunch they buy you. They're very careful to let you know how important you are to them by choosing a restaurant like Faust, and letting you order whatever you want.'

When I left Stan, I was still hungry. I went back to my hotel and made a sandwich. It was a vegetable sandwich, consisting of toasted mushrooms and grilled onions and roasted peppers on white bread with plenty of mustard and salt. It was good. These sandwiches were always good, because they reminded me of my childhood, which felt safe. Some of the best tasting things I could eat now that I was an adult were things that didn't really taste very good at all, except that they reminded me of my childhood and so they tasted safe.

One of those was oatmeal. One of those was a vegetable sandwich, which my mother had probably learned to make when meat was harder to find, after the war. One of those was what we called 'Chinese food', though it wasn't Chinese food at all. It wasn't even *like* Chinese food. It didn't look like Chinese food, and it definitely didn't taste like Chinese food. I don't know what was in it. I think 'Chinese food' was just its nickname, and I was never able to discover, before my mother died, exactly what it was or where it came from.

It felt safe, but I couldn't replicate it. So sometimes when I was feeling down I would eat actual Chinese food, and that would give me solace just because it shared a name with 'Chinese food'.

The hotel we lived in – the Avondale – was originally built as apartments, and because it offered small rooms with very moderate toilet facilities – in some cases you had to take a bath in the sink – it became a favorite habitation of bit players, acrobatic dancers, bottom-bill unicyclists and 'specialty artists' like Rubber Legs McKendrie. It suited people with little means who needed somewhere to stay.

Now it was called a hotel, although it didn't offer rooms by the night. Most residents of the Avondale were in transition. They were at the beginning of something, or something in their lives was coming to an end. Some of us were hopefuls, like me. Some were at the end of careers that had peaked some time before, or had never quite taken off.

I lay on my bed and decided a nap would be good for me, and if it wasn't, well, it would feel nice anyway. I was a great lover of the afternoon nap. I could always sleep after eating lunch, and nothing gave me greater pleasure. I loved how my thoughts would go dreamy and start to make no sense. Sense was so exhausting, and I loved watching it slowly drift away from me.

The cheap curtains in my room billowed and the sun behind them was bright outside.

I woke. The phone was ringing.

It was in the hall. It was always for me. No one else ever received any phone calls.

'Hello?' It was my agent, Samuel Greene. He was not Jewish. He was the only non-Jewish agent in Hollywood, as far as I knew. I think he was an apostate Mormon.

'I got a screen test for you tomorrow. You're gonna do your screen test, and then I'm gonna take you to lunch. How does that sound? You got a favorite place?'

'Faust.'

'Ha! How do you know about that place? I knew you were special. I'm gonna make something outa you. I fuckin' swear it! I don't care where the hell you came from, I'm gonna make something outa you! And I'm gonna take you to Faust. But listen, you gotta pass the screen test, OK?'

'Pass it?'

'I mean you gotta get the show. You promise? You promise you fucking no good piece of shit you?'

'I promise. What's the show?'

'It's called *The Joneses*. That's the title. It's about an all-American fuckin' family who are just adorable and get into zany scrapes but always learn from their mistakes and above all, they love each other very fuckin' much.'

'Who do I play?'

'You play Bobby Jones, a high school kid – yeah, I know, you're too old, but they want to see you anyway – who creates hilarious new problems in addition to the ones he's already got, but he has a heart of gold and a winning smile and he's a big fat fuckin' sweetheart who every mother is gonna wish was her own and every teenage girl is gonna have up on her wall.'

THE JONESES

I hung up the phone and practiced my winning smile in front of the mirror.

The next day, I tried my very best not to dress up or down. I went to the production studio on Highland. I never before had an audition where there were so many people watching me. There were at least twelve. I didn't even know who they all were.

After they were finished with me, I said goodbye, and went out the door to find Sammy in the foyer. He was pacing, smoking a menthol.

'What did they say?'

'Nothing.'

'Did it feel like you got it?'

'What does that feel like?'

'Don't be a smart ass. Let's go to lunch. That's how it should feel. Eating at Faust: that's how it should feel.'

We walked to Faust. Nobody walks in Los Angeles, but Faust was only three minutes away, over on Sunset Boulevard.

The maitre d' knew Sammy. We got a booth in the inner circle. I could tell it was a good seat.

There were Venetian lanterns hanging over our heads, making the space glow. Everything was soft and it felt safe.

Faust had specialties, but none was as famous as the chili con carne. 'Their chili is so famous,' Sammy said, 'that when Elizabeth Taylor was shooting *Cleopatra*, she had Faust send chili every day – every fuckin' day! – to the set. And that was in Egypt!' He paused, watching me, allowing this information to settle. 'So... what are you having?'

'The chili.'

'You want a martini?'

I'd never had a martini before. It felt like a grown-up drink.

'Yeah. Let's have a martini.'

'Two martinis!'

After lunch, I went back to my room at the Avondale and took a nap. I dreamt about being Bobby Jones. For once I actually dreamt about the thing that occupied my waking mind. I dreamt feelings rather than facts. In the dream I was shooting *The Joneses*, and I was playing Bobby Jones. But that was just the activity of the dream. What I really dreamt of was a fullness. I felt occupied, precise, and filled out to the right size. I knew what to do in each moment of the dream. There was no hesitation. I was solid. I was home.

I woke up in the morning and I rang Sammy myself.

'You got it.'

'I got it?'

'You got it, you fuck.'

'So why didn't you ring?' I don't know why I said that.

Now Sammy laughed out loud. 'I'm waiting for the first script and the shooting schedule. You got it, you motherfucker. You're Bobby Jones.'

My thoughts were distant. 'How—'

'Long?'

'Yeah.'

'Will you have to—'

'Yeah.'

'I don't know. Stay close to the phone.'

'Stay—'

'Naw, go out. You know, you better go out and enjoy the world while nobody knows who you are. Because that's not going to last.'

Something was happening – I knew that much – but I decided not to figure out what it was just yet.

I turned and saw Stan was waiting for me. 'Anything new?'

'I ate at Faust.'

'You did?'

We went downstairs and got in my car. I'd promised to drive Stan to an audition for a play that paid nothing in a fifty-seat theatre. We didn't talk much about work. His part in the film had been cut.

He wanted to know what I'd eaten at Faust. I lied. I told him I'd had a steak and fries, and a beer. He was quiet. He knew I was lying. He probably thought I was lying about having lunch at Faust. I didn't describe the interior. I didn't want to prove to him I'd eaten there.

I wanted him to think I was lying. I was playing someone smaller than I was, and I was enjoying it. I knew I had only a short time to enjoy him in the old way.

THE JONESES

I felt my friendship with Stan changing in the car, at that moment, and not because I was now Bobby Jones. It was nothing to do with the show. It was because I couldn't tell him what I'd eaten at Faust.

The truth is, I could have ordered anything – anything *flambé*, anything *au jus*. But I wanted the chili. I wanted the chili because you could eat food at any time, and the chili wasn't just food. It was something more than just itself. It was a star on the Walk of Fame. It was history. Yes it tasted good. And it tasted better because my agent Sammy was smiling at me, smiling at every spoonful I ate, like my eating was feeding *him*. Yes it tasted good. I was hungry so it tasted good, and it felt good. But more of me was hungry than the thing that could eat that chili, and more of me was eating that chili than just the part of me that could eat.

Craig Warner has received a number of award nominations for his television, film, and theatre work, including BAFTA, Writers' Guild and Broadcasting Press Guild awards, among others. His play *Strangers on a Train*, based on Patricia Highsmith's novel, recently enjoyed a successful run in the West End.

STEPHANIE YE

First Light From
the Farthest Star

The prologue to a novel

THE UNIVERSE IS ENDING AND IF I DON'T HURRY, I'LL MISS MY CHANCE TO KILL ASTER. The sky is filling in with stars, the way rust encrusts a sheet of iron. At the dock, I procure a speedboat, slicing its mooring ropes with my lanser. The owner is nowhere to be seen, his rental kiosk maglocked, like all the other stalls up and down the empty promenade. Spray-painted in red on the metal shutter, in incongruously elegant copperplate script, are the words 'Closed Forever'. Next to it, a postcard-sized cardboard sign, the laminate peeling at the corners, reads 'Back At:'; the sun-bleached plastic hands of the printed clockface below point at 5.40. Morning or evening? It doesn't matter. The sun burned out on Thursday and, anyway, we've long stopped bothering to keep time – it just keeps running out.

I put the boat into drive and steer it out of the harbour. Up north, the ice covers all, but here at the edge of the equator the cold is still crisp, The Pore's eternal summer finally falling into winter. A few snowflakes dance across my face, but as I get out to sea there's nothing but the wind on my skin, salt skimming my lips. The water is choppy, the waves surging then collapsing just as their tips catch the starlight. There's hardly any empty sky left. They say that when the end comes, the sky will be completely white. We will see the light from the farthest stars, from every single star that was ever born. Truly the event of a lifetime, an out-of-this-world experience, a sight to end all sights. I've heard all the apocalypse jokes by now.

The lights of the promenade are a faint glow on the horizon when I hear the music. It is frenzied yet fragile, the sound of ice cracking as it melts. I am convinced it comes from the stars. Then I see the seaship. Its approaching mass grows brighter and brighter as if, like the sky, it were being filled in with stars. The music clarifies itself as a waltz, played by a string ensemble. I see the couples with their shimmering clothing and glistening faces on the heated deck, swirling about each other in 3/4 time. I can almost smell the wine and the perfume. This must be one of the more expensive 'last-night-of-the-world' parties. It's not like people have anything else to save up for.

The yacht passes me. My little boat rocks in its wake as I stare at the brilliant spot shrinking in the distance. My ears strain to hold on to the rumble of the cello, but all I can hear are the waves. I think about the unfathomable fathoms beneath that glittering surface that will never be bothered by starlight.

I'm heading for a lighthouse that doesn't have a light. No matter: the stars are enough to steer by. The island Aster lives on is really a glorified rock, albeit a well-fortified one with, knowing Aster, all the creature comforts that money and modern technology can provide. Not a bad way to spend the rest of your days, though, if circumstances were otherwise, I wouldn't choose to spend the rest of my days with Aster. Hell, I wouldn't choose to spend any day with Aster.

It looms before me now. Satumu Island is flat and squat like a manta ray. Its lighthouse is bone white and laced with cracks. In this instant, I can feel Aster's presence so strongly, as if he were staring at me. Maybe he is staring at me, alone in his lighthouse. He is waiting for me in his lighthouse on his rock and I am in my boat in the sea, speeding towards him. And everyone else is on that ever-distant yacht, dancing their way to the end.

I reach the island. I hastily dock the speedboat. I don't bother to secure it: I won't be using it again. My skin is tingling and my heart is racing as I clamber onto the pier. Its weathered wood is pale gold in the starlight, but the jungle beyond is dark and, as the roar of the ocean falls away, peculiarly quiet. The lighthouse is on the other side of the island, the other side of that tangle, where the land falls sharply into the sea in a jumble of rocks and other broken pieces of itself. There is a concrete path snaking its way through the jungle's primaeval gloom and I take it. The salt of the sea has worked its way into my nostrils, but its bracing scent is soon overpowered by the odour of vegetation, slimy and physical and constrictive.

I know it cannot be far, but I cannot see the lighthouse, only the veil of leaves above me. Something crunches as I step on it. In the scant starlight that makes its way through the canopy, I can see that the path is dotted with small, ovoid objects, like seed pods. Then I realise that they are crickets, the crickets whose screams are missing from the jungle. The insects are motionless, dead perhaps or just in cryogenic sleep. It is colder than it's ever been, and it will only get colder still.

Maybe fifteen minutes, maybe fifty, then I begin once again to hear the pounding of the waves, though the jungle shows no sign of ending. Or maybe it's just the roar of blood in my ears. My heart is hammering imperiously against my breastbone, beneath the pocket containing the book that is my passport to this island, which holds the text so important to Aster that he is finally allowing me to come close. I would say that I hope this decision is his hamartia, except of course I do not see him as the tragic hero of this story.

The lighthouse is suddenly before me, gleaming softly like pallid flesh. Up close, I see that what I had thought were cracks are actually vines, clinging to the curved stone with fat, translucent fingers. I think of castle towers in timeless tales, hiding imprisoned princesses in their crowns. But I face no dragons or witches' spells, just a smooth metal door set seamlessly into the ancient wall. It emits a beep as I stand before it, but does not open. Then a muffled pop and, to the right of the doorway, a drawer drops slowly open. An illuminated sign inside the cavity in the shape of a lanser makes it clear what I have to surrender to gain admission. I place my weapon in the cavity and the door beeps again, scanning me once more. Then it slides open with a hiss.

Aster must know I've arrived. He must be thinking of me as I ascend the helix staircase, my feet thudding dully on the metal, the only light the feebly glowing strips set into the hypotenuse of each triangular step. He must be thinking, like me, of how to act when we finally meet again, soon, after all this time. He must be thinking of me thinking about him.

FIRST LIGHT FROM THE FARTHEST STAR

I cannot see my hands before me as I grope my way upwards. The interior wall is smooth as glass; it's freezing and palpably sterile, and I imagine my fingers leaving warm smears of DNA, marking my passage even after the surface has once again cooled over. My breathing seems to echo about me, thrown back from the cavern above, the abyss below. I am counting, then I realise I've already lost track of the number of steps I've taken. I am sure Aster is counting, that he knows how many more steps I have to go.

I feel my irises clench as all at once I'm surrounded by light. Starlight is streaming in through the massive glass windows of the lantern room, filling the emptiness of the empty space. It swells up against the high domed ceiling; it turns the bare blank floor into a moonscape. I shut my eyes, open them again. I am dazzled, giddily elated by all that light. It is almost as an afterthought that I perceive the too-slight figure at the far side of the room.

Aster steps forward and the glare of the stars illuminates, unexpectedly, the face that I've most longed to see.

Stephanie Ye is writing a literary science fiction novel inspired by the cross-dressing woman warrior Hua Mulan. Her stories have appeared in publications including *Esquire, Mascara Literary Review* and *Best New Singaporean Short Stories*. She was born in Singapore, attended college in Chicago, and at UEA holds a Creative Writing International Scholarship.

CHRISTOPHER YOUNG

The System of Locks

An extract from a novel

IN THE FOYER OF THE ROYAL FESTIVAL HALL, EVERY SURFACE HAD BEEN DECKED in chocolatier tones of purple and orange; narrow silver-wire structures were dotted across a red carpet floor, supporting bouquets of white roses, lady-slipper orchids and white palm leaves. Above Julia, the ceiling was sprinkled with winking LEDs, a bright-burning electronic cosmos. Maroon satin drapes, backlit by evening light, erased the Thames from view. The guests were scheduled to arrive at six.

Julia stood in front of the drapes, a tray of twenty white wine glasses balanced on her open palms. When you worked trays, white wine was not the worst drink to be given – but everyone wanted to be serving champagne: guests snapped it up at a pace, giving you the chance to rest your muscles and work some life back into your arms, as you headed to the bar for a restock. Also, the glasses were smaller – they made for a lighter tray overall.

Fanny, Fabricio, Pavel, Sara and Katja were on champagne. Julia shot Pavel a look across the hall. Probably the strongest person on staff and he'd been given champagne. What's more, he was cheating, holding his tray about waist-level, transferring the weight to his belt buckle. He smiled back. Pavel's row of traywaiters was arranged in front of a large canvas banner, which sported the event logo: a golden clapperboard, embellished with a single rose. Underneath it was the slogan, flamboyantly typeset: 'The Distinction in Television Awards: Lights, Camera, Passion.'

Beneath her blouse Julia felt stifled. The air was thick. Across her back, pinpricks of sweat began to adhere to her shirt.

THE SYSTEM OF LOCKS

The room started to fill with artificial smoke, which spread the coloured spotlight beams in the air, like Chinese fans.

Red wine was the worst drink to be assigned. It came in the largest glass, and no one touched it. It was a mealtime drink, a bad fit with lipstick. You could be holding red for an hour without someone taking a glass, lightening the load. Tonight the new girl – Ana or Anya, Julia couldn't remember – was on it. She was tiny, birdlike, next to Julia. Her tray was already beginning to shake.

Julia sniffed. There'd been a needling in her sinuses since Robbie had come around the staff area, tilting their heads upwards and spraying them with some type of musk. Julia fought back the urge to sneeze. The guests were beginning to trickle in.

Robbie burst through the staff entrance. He was a man of round edges – soft-shouldered, pudding-jowled and puppyish. He looked younger than Julia, and was. Spitting the occasional word into a walkie-talkie, he made his way along her row. Julia smirked at the quick, snapping gait, the way he held his walkie-talkie at a cocked angle – he was trying to look like a slick operator, but Julia was under no illusions. She'd seen him once outside Tower Hill station before a job, sucking down a cigarette as if it were his last. He hated his work as much as anyone.

From her left, Julia heard a sigh. She turned to see Ana trembling, the glasses on her tray rattling like the dining car of an old Hollywood train. Watching her, she felt the weight of the tray in her own hands, the dampness of her palms, the hardening of her biceps. The sweat on her brow flashed cold. They couldn't have been on trays for longer than ten minutes.

Robbie drew up in front of her.

'All right Jules? Ready?'

Jules. She hated that Robbie could remember her name. It meant that she was on his speed dial for any odd jobs or favours that needed doing.

'Yeah, ready.' Julia made a quick assessment. If she could draw Robbie's attention to Ana's struggles, he might be convinced to put Pavel and some of the other boys on wine. If there was a reshuffle she could land herself a champagne tray. She tilted her head towards Ana. 'You should let her switch trays though. I think she needs to be on champagne.'

Robbie fixed Ana with a stare.

'What's this? You can't do the red?'

Eyes wide, Ana looked at Robbie, at Julia, then back at Robbie. She gulped.

'It's not actually complicated, you know.' His voice was low, a murmur. 'Not really brain surgery, is it, holding a tray?'

'It's fine. I'm OK.'

'No I don't think so,' Julia cut in, watching Ana's arms and feeling her own, 'look at the shaking.'

Julia tried to pass Ana a smile of consolation, conspiracy. As if she had everything all under control.

Robbie wiped his brow. Groaned.

'Fuck's sake. Right, Jules, give me your tray.'

Julia passed her tray to Robbie and for a moment her arms felt blessed.

'Right, now you,' he said, turning to the girl, 'give those to her.'

The girl transferred her tray onto Julia's hands, which dipped under the weight. The underside of the tray was slick with sweat.

'Now take these,' Robbie handed the tray to Ana and a tremor of her muscles set the glasses chiming.

'Just stand there, smile, and remember that I'm really, really fucking busy. Don't bother me unless it's an emergency – clear?'

Ana nodded. Julia bit her lip. She scanned the room: the first guests were dignitaries, producers, press. No one recognisable. They helped themselves happily to champagne. Julia tried to catch Pavel's eye again, but he didn't notice.

The drape behind Julia lost its warmth as day passed into evening. As Julia had feared, no one was taking the red. She had shifted the tray in her hands so that it was now clamped by her thumbs. Training forbade it – people didn't want a thumb near their glass – but it helped stop the shaking. She felt the lactic acid build in her muscles, the chemical burn, the heat beneath her sleeves.

The arrivals turned from industry insiders to public faces: Johnny Myles, the soap actor, sprang into the reception, strikingly short and sporting a tan that turned almost terracotta under the foyer lights. A dress of some peacock-down fabric clung to every angle of 'it girl' Gwynevere James, while Sir Marcus

THE SYSTEM OF LOCKS

Forshaw made Ana's night by sweeping up two glasses of Chardonnay and thanking her until she blushed. Julia watched the feather boa trail down the back of his jacket, an expensive-looking tweed. She had worn Pat's long coat to work that morning, an ageing Barbour. It covered her to the knees in the dark walk to the bus station. Recently, she had been able to appreciate the silence of being awake before the others, the feeling of having stolen time on the world around. The vulnerable quality of every shop face and lamp post. The stillness of the mornings. Without Pat she had time, and she still hadn't figured out how to use it, how to make it work, how to make it pass.

Soon the foyer was full. Well-tailored shoulders rubbed up against dagger-blade dresses, all taking calculated sips of champagne. Most of the tray waiters had been moved to clearing duty, and were drifting through the crowd like shadows. Ana had gone to the bar for a restock, and had not come back.

Julia was still on trays.

The acid ache had spread outwards from her biceps, sweeping down to her fingertips. Her arms were heavy. Knots of muscle screwed tight across her back like a system of locks. No one was taking the wine. She felt her tray shaking, saw the wineglasses trembling at their dark hemispheres. No one was taking the wine. She couldn't remember how long she'd been there: forty-five minutes, maybe an hour. She focused on anything she could: the faces, the names – there was Angus Wright, Izzie Baker, Ronnie Bergkamp; the top forty playlist, restyled as lounge jazz for a cultivated diffidence. Thoughts of Pat came to her, his body stiff on cold linoleum, the dark fluids diluting in the shower-spray. When they released her nothing changed: no one was taking the wine.

She was eyeing the bar – an island of glassware, backlit in phasing violets, azures, emeralds – when a small, wiry man in a leather jacket stopped in front of her. He wore a quizzical expression, a half-grin, a humour to his eyes. She recognised him from a television talent show. A singer.

'What's that you got there?' His accent was unmistakably north western. Liverpool, Julia guessed.

'Oh, this is a Californian Merlot, from Blackstone Winery.'

The importance of mentioning the sponsor names had been drilled into them.

'Fancy that.' His smile morphed into a frown. 'Are you OK? You're shaking.'

'Oh, don't worry. I'm fine thanks. I'm used to it.'

'That looks heavy.'

'I'm used to it.'

'Fuck. How long have you been working here?'

Julia tried to smile. 'What time is it?'

'Seven.'

'Fourteen hours.'

The man sucked his teeth, looked downwards.

'Shit. Well, let me have one of those. Give me two.'

He plucked two shivering glasses from Julia's tray, and though the relief was not great, it was something. Julia took a breath, and nodded her thanks.

'Cheers,' he said.

The music faded to nothing as an announcement came over the PA system.

Ladies and gentlemen, we would like to ask you to please start making your way to the auditorium, where tonight's ceremony is about to begin...

'Better be off then,' he said, and made to turn.

Please be advised that drinks are not permitted in the auditorium.

He rolled his eyes at her and slowly, deliberately, poured the contents of the wine glasses into a nearby flower arrangement. Returning the empty glasses to her tray, he grinned:

'Good luck with it.'

Christopher Young, 24, was born in Twickenham. He has been shortlisted for the 2008 Fish International Short Story Award, and has written for the *Times Literary Supplement* and the *New York Daily News*. He is currently working on his first novel, about the unseen side of luxury events.

SARAH YOUNG

Black Flag

An extract from a novel following a photojournalist through the Middle East and New Zealand during the 2011 Arab Spring uprisings and Christchurch earthquake.

SHE WALKS ALONG THE SAND BESIDE THE ROAD, MAKING SURE THE CAMERA IS HIDDEN. The sweat-soaked strap is heavy around her neck, chafing the sliver of bare skin occasionally exposed by the hot wind. She can feel something building. Light disintegrating into purple haze, sand clouds boiling in the distance, horizon invisible. Houses seem empty, electrical wiring hanging down patchily painted walls, pipes rusting, leaking, exposed. Sprawling graffiti. The side of Bahrain she is not supposed to see.

Barren is the only word. Dust on her tongue, dirt in her system, sand in her veins. No – sand is too discreet, too full of running movement, able to be trickled from hand to hand, cleanly changing shape. That's Dubai. Bahrain is clinging, cloying, soft dust; everything shot through a dirty lens.

At least there are some people around here though. Old men playing chess on a table under a burnt tree, terse and urgent voices cracking out of their portable radio into the silence. A small boy inching his way down a broken slide in a playground encased in barbed wire. Over the road, older boys throw a ball to each other on a concrete soccer pitch with rusting goalposts, taunting the smallest who jumps desperately with arms held straight above his head.

When she walked out of the hotel earlier, under the full glare of a sun erasing every surface to white, the business district was empty. A few skyscrapers stretching above squat concrete buildings into the blue, the odd statue here and there. A different kind of fake, rougher, like a child's attempt at forgery; a toy city without inhabitants, everyone put to sleep by a wicked witch.

People come out at night, a man sweeping the bare courtyard of the museum told her. Like rats.

She wants to get her camera out now, she wants to get at this, this strange sense of life still going on, even if it is a muted life, a life holding its breath as it goes about its daily tasks, surreptitiously preparing for the main event. She feels naked without the lens before her face. That passport to invisibility, to being allowed to stare. Not here though. A camera means a different thing. Can't risk it, not yet.

She can still feel Mark's touch from this morning. What is he doing now? Cleaning his gun? Poring over maps? She has no idea. Even his text earlier as he walked to the base seemed to come from a voice she didn't understand.

Just saw a body in the street. Good omen?

She failed to see how. He neglected to give her the details she wanted – age, gender, manner of death, where – so instead, as she lay in the hotel bed, she had to consider all the scenarios, an endless array of dead people draped over various parts of the city, until she couldn't handle being in that room any longer. But he won't know. She'll be back before him.

The road turns. Ahead is the roundabout with its strange monument, six sails joining to hold a pearl. Looks more like six ribs to her, bones bereft of flesh, pulled out from their cage formation, leaning against each other like a tepee curving out widely to the base. The ribs touch just before the top, where they unfurl again slightly, a blooming flower of bones, petals opening up to the sun to reveal the white ball inside. This is where the protest is supposed to begin. And end? She hasn't really thought about that yet.

A line of policemen sit in deckchairs beside a black Humvee, legs splayed, AK47s across their laps, some listening to earphones, others staring up into the sky. She lowers her head, readjusts her scarf over the camera. Lucky to be here, really. Plenty of reasons why she shouldn't be here at all.

They detained her immediately upon arrival. Over there, they said, directing her to the chairs lining the wall outside the customs office. Wait.

She sat, shaking hands hidden beneath her bag, occasionally wiping her palms on her legs. I'm not here as a journalist, she repeated, as a man passed her another form to fill in.

As the last of her planeload was processed, one of the bored-looking officials in white sat down beside her, stomach bulging, stretching his legs and sandalled feet out with a sigh. They struck up a stilted conversation covering the important questions: how far away was New Zealand, did they really keep kangaroos for pets, oh that was Australia, right, but did she still know if their tails could actually kill a man, anyway why was she living in Dubai, had she been to Bahrain before, did she like their national museum? Finally, he asked why she was here. Really.

She gave the lines, and he smiled. Sat back, and lit a cigarette, right there under the non-smoking sign.

Engaged huh? Then you go back and it's all done. Finito. Yeah? He raised his eyebrow as he took another drag, and smiled again, a knowing, sly smile. I've seen you before, that smile said. I've seen plenty of girls like you. She considered trying to maintain her front, but could see there was no point. Laughed, shrugged. Tried to look unbothered, bored even. Wished she had worn a slightly longer dress. Supposed at least if he felt he'd seen through one lie, he might not go looking for another.

He stayed there beside her, lit up another cigarette, pattered on about restaurants she should go to, local food she should try. No one seemed bothered by his smoking. She wanted to light one too, but no. Obviously not. The people who had also been held back on her flight – a pregnant Sudanese woman, an American businessman, and an old man who looked African too, perhaps – were let go. People coming through the gates from the next flight, and the next, stared at her. She felt like a criminal, every blemish exposed under those cold fluorescent lights.

Occasionally the guy leaned his head around the door into the small office where his higher-ranking colleagues were Googling her name and previous work. Let the Kiwi girl go. She's all right. They'd reply in a short burst of Arabic, and he'd waggle his head, suck on his smoke. All right, all right. He'd try again a few minutes later. They kept talking. He asked her about

BLACK FLAG

Dubai. Horrible place, yeah? She gave a noncommittal shrug. He nodded, understood. She liked him. It was probably the most genuine conversation she'd had with a stranger in months.

They called her in twice. Who you work for? Why your camera? Are you doing a story? Each time she gave them the same answers, and they sent her out again. Then called her back in. Give us your fiancé's number. We will ring him.

Half an hour later, a slim young man in a cream kandura held out her passport. You can go, he muttered, and walked off. The guy with the stamp slammed it down, eyes grinning.

She heads down the side street behind the cops. A tall man in black resting against a wall appraises her slowly while speaking into his phone. Usually she's pretty good at reading people; you didn't grow up the way she had and not be. But not this guy. Not those eyes. Another young man swerves slowly down the road on his bike, eating a chocolate bar from one hand, and stops to speak briefly with the man on the phone. She can smell burning meat. Black flags reach from windows above her, creating a moving, chequered ceiling of sky. She wonders if she should be here. This street feels different. She should know what those flags mean. But she hasn't exactly had the time. Everything happened so fast.

She tips the last of her water into her mouth, looks back at the row of policemen underneath the deepening purple sky. Yes. It's building. She imagines the people cooking that meat, hiding away in clouds of smoke inside these shells. Others collecting paving stones peeled from roads and rocks slipped into pockets earlier in the day, filling old glass Coke bottles with petrol and kerosene. T-shirts torn up into rags, balaclavas fashioned from large jersey sleeves, ragged eye diamonds cut with knives. Lopsided slogans scrawled across the backs of stolen real estate signs, more of these black flags being made, the humming of isolated sewing machines reaching out to join in the growing darkness above.

Preparations conducted in silence, unseen but still felt; an invisible network slowly gathering force. She turns back. The policemen look bored, oblivious to these ghosts of the future marching towards them. She wants to raise her lens again. But not now, not yet. Not with those blank eyes still idly assessing her, flicking from her ankles to her chest, resting briefly on her face, and then back again. She wipes the sweat from the back of her neck. Is she ready for this? Really? She thinks of the news article Mark sent her, with the photo of the girl in the red dress. Turkey. Or maybe Greece. Long dark hair flying, body twisting in the air in front of a backdrop of plastic police shields, face scrunched up to avoid the fine mist coming towards her, the photo capturing the moment before impact, the moment before spray hit skin, eyes, mouth, nose. Even as she turned her face, that girl was defiant. *Looks kind of like you*, he wrote.

But that isn't her role. She isn't that girl. Wouldn't know how to fight if she tried. She looks at her watch. Almost six. Mark said seven, didn't he? They work odd hours. She feels the same surprise she always feels when she suddenly remembers he is a navy man. A captain. No, a riverine captain. Combat warfare. *We're trained to kill.* That video, taken on someone's phone, he sent her a few weeks back – *This is what we really do. What people don't realise, or don't want to know. All that stuff they told you when you visited – that was bullshit. This is it. The real deal.* Machine gun bullets rupturing the air, the roar of the jetboat racing up the brown river, Mark's voice directing his guys, swearing, getting lost amongst their shouted replies, she couldn't tell which one he was, they all looked the same in their helmets, dark sunglasses, bullet-proof vests. Raw energy reverberating around the boat and then pouring into the jungle, more shouting, more bullets, rough and urgent and short against the lazy, waving electric chords of the Alice in Chains soundtrack. *Rooster.* Like the tattoos on the top of their right feet. *Cock on the right, never lose a fight. Pig on the knee, safety at sea.* Some had crosses on the bottom of their feet to keep the sharks away too, he said.

The fear, revulsion and excitement she felt as she watched it, as she replayed the song afterwards, trying to imagine him in what looked to her only like Conrad's *Heart of Darkness*. A fiction. And of course it wasn't real. It was a training exercise. But it was training for *something*, something that for all she knew had already happened.

She heads back towards the main road, wondering again who this man really is, this man who can order the firing of machine guns into something or someone he can't even see, this man she kissed for the first time in an alleyway only a month ago. And who, really, he thinks she is.

Sarah Young is a New Zealand journalist who has worked in Indonesia and the United Arab Emirates. She is the recipient of the 2013/14 UEA Man Booker Scholarship, and is working on a novel and a set of linked novellas.